Literary Criticism: An Autopsy

CRITICAL AUTHORS & ISSUES

Josué Harari, Series Editor

A complete list of books in the series
is available from the publisher.

Literary Criticism: An Autopsy

Mark Bauerlein

PENN

University of Pennsylvania Press

Philadelphia

Copyright © 1997 University of Pennsylvania Press
All rights reserved
Printed in the United States of America on acid-free paper

10 9 8 7 6 5 4 3 2 1

Published by
University of Pennsylvania Press
Philadelphia, Pennsylvania 19104-6097

Library of Congress Cataloging-in-Publication Data

Bauerlein, Mark.
    Literary criticism, an autopsy / Mark Bauerlein.
        p.   cm.
    ISBN 0-8122-3411-1 (alk. paper)
    1. Criticism.   I. Title.
PN81.B387   1997
801'.95—dc21   97-14199
                                               CIP

to
Eve-Alice Roustang

Contents

Preface

In 1994, at an English department meeting at Emory University, I found myself in the middle of a debate over future staffing needs. Naturally, the faculty members all had varying, though mutually respectful opinions. Some thought we should fill historical gaps in our curriculum with entry-level period specialists. Others pushed for a distinguished scholar in any field to strengthen the research credentials of the graduate program. Another opted for a composition specialist to waylay the adjunct hiring we have to undergo every semester. Yet another suggested a computer expert to bring us all technologically up to date.

Though we disagreed about the relative merits of each proposal, we admitted each one as having some measure of justification. Everyone recognized a rationale behind each idea being thrown around the table and understood that the department's final choice was a matter of deciding on the priority of one proposal over another, not accepting one and rejecting the others. We merely had to rank them in terms of urgency. But, as the colloquy proceeded, one colleague offered a general comment that introduced a new concern. He said, "I think we should all realize that the world has changed drastically in the last twenty years and that we should think about how we as a department and as individual scholars and teachers are going to represent those changes." A lull followed this statement, as if the other faculty members were thinking about how to assimilate Professor X's wake-up call to the issue at hand. Maybe X intended his point as a reproof to some of the conservative opinions expressed ("We need a straightforward Miltonist"). Perhaps it was meant as support for arguments for a less traditionally defined scholar, a postcolonialist or a cultural critic, for example. Or perhaps X was impatient with the intradepartmental focus of the discussion and wanted to open it to some broader social considerations. In any case, the conversation picked up again, but I do not remember what course it took. I was too absorbed in turning over in my mind X's sentence, particularly the words "should," "realize," "world," and, above all, "represent." They expressed what I thought was an inscrutable conception, namely, that the English department and its members should represent the world and that this goal was not so much an institutional definition as an ethical obligation. I assumed X's idea that professors should represent world change meant not only that literature programs should hire women and minorities and encourage serious study of literature by women and minorities. If that were the case, X could have said so explicitly and received universal support. But instead, X offered a general reminder of our representational task, kept his statement at the level of vague commandment, with a touch of *ressentiment* thrown in. As such, X's sentence came off as an application of the representational goal to all disciplinary acts, not to just hiring practices.

This is what threw me. Representation of the world here amounted to a professional imperative, a guiding motive professors should live and work by. I was not quite sure what "representation" signified (demographic equivalence of department and society? advocacy of certain groups' interests? narration of certain individuals' experience?), but I nevertheless felt its coercive pull. To X, at least, our justification as scholars and teachers came down to this one duty. It was an injunction that professors submit their writing, pedagogy, and administrative work to representing the world lying beyond the walls of academia. Representation should direct canon formation, course offerings, PhD exams, composition instruction, readings of poems, tenure evaluations, and so on. This extramural idea carried all the weight of a moral precept, a base ethical criterion overriding professional considerations and local circumstances, such as a department's weakness in this or that historical area or its poor record of graduate placement.

X's proposition was quietly forceful and conceptually simple. But, in asserting representation as the base criterion for judging research and teaching, the statement raised enormous logistical problems. Though the substitution of representation for other disciplinary criteria was easy to conceive, how were we supposed to implement it? In drawing a profile of a prospective job candidate, how should representation figure? Should we single out scholars whose methods were squarely sociological? Or should we select scholars whose work broached recent cultural formations like postmodernism? Once we accepted a representation criterion, what further guidelines could we invoke? What disciplinary protocols, investigative methods, and studied objects went along with the representational mandate? So long as literary study involved the research into and teaching of reading and writing skills, literary history, and textual interpretation, its methodological parameters and canons of evaluation were commonly understood, though debatable. The purpose of composition instruction was to improve students' writing. An English major was designed to teach students a literary canon and show them methods of analyzing it. Scholarly articles on works of literature proposed to detail those works' style and semantics. But what was the end of representation? What norms and standards went along with it? What was its canon, its subject matter? What distinguished a good representation from a bad one? What forms of training would lead students toward the good ones? How did my training in literary history and textual interpretation qualify me to be a representative?

Two weeks later, before I had begun to answer any of these questions, I found myself in another situation that left me professionally confused. A friend running a Romanticism conference asked me to chair a panel on "Romantic Legacies" and to serve as its respondent. I begged off, outwardly citing my ignorance of the field's current scholarship and inwardly dreading getting involved in another dismal conference exercise. He countered that he had nobody else to do it and I relented. He promised to have the panelists send me their papers the following week. The confusion arose when I got the first paper from Scholar Y and sat down to read it. The first sentence read, "This paper will examine the convergence of Romantic and homoerotic gender discourses in the 19th and 20th centuries." In the succeeding paragraphs, Y paraphrased some of Walt Whitman's *Calamus* poems, summed up repressive nineteenth-century attitudes toward sexuality, invoked Jean Baudrillard's concept of simulation, paraphrased sections of Hart Crane's *The Bridge*, countered Harold Bloom's conflictual model of poetic influence with a Whitmanian "comradeship" model, analyzed Allen Ginsberg's "A Supermarket in California," described post-World War II urban alienation, and finally indicated that in these issues could be found a resolution to the subject-object dichotomy created by Kant. All this in fourteen pages. When I checked the accompanying vita to see where such erudition and critical mastery came from, I saw that Y graduated from high school in 1993, was a junior at a large midwestern university, and had already delivered two conference papers earlier in the year.

A closer look at Y's paper left no doubt that his overblown effort did not qualify as serious scholarship. The paper's tepid thesis— "there is a lineage of post-Romantic homoerotic poetry"—was largely undemonstrated, for five poems do not a tradition make. The paper's critical terms—"convergence," "simulation," "homo-erotic"—remained uncontextualized. The historical generaliza-tions—"Whitman's society censured him for his homoeroticism" —had no documentation to back them up (and were, in this case, wrong). But although the paper lacked anything resembling a coherent methodology, it did possess in abundance much of the language of contemporary criticism. Though he did not bother to define his critical terms, Scholar Y sprinkled his sentences gener-ously with "discourse," "contestation," "gender," "hegemonic," "patriarchal," "transgressive," and the like. The diction was wholly familiar and clichéd. Though his phrasings and epithets often lacked a clear referent—just what is "a convergence of Roman-tic and homoerotic gender discourses"?—the words Y chose ap-parently carried enough institutional echoes to warrant their un-supported use. Somewhere along the line, perhaps through a misguided undergraduate mentor, Y had imbibed a professional lingo, a lexicon and a usage that supposedly could stand on its own without methodological backup. The mere mention of these words was sufficient. Any further clarification of them (philologi-cal, historical, Whitmanian) was superfluous.

As I pondered how to respond to the paper, what troubled me was this: not that it failed to employ sound research methods, but that it had no interest in employing them. Y had come to under-stand scholarly work as a superficial mimesis, not as a disciplinary inquiry with its own canons of logic, evidence, historiography, and interpretation. Y mimicked the language of criticism with a canny facility—and did nothing more. Y announced Whitman's, Crane's, and Ginsberg's homoeroticism, but he did not fulfill his claim to explore the convergence of discourses. He did not reconstruct the historical and biographical particulars of their homoeroticism. He did not recount the homophobia they faced. He did not even prove that Crane and Ginsberg read the *Calamus* poems. I had presumed that these were standard procedures for working up a literary genealogy. But for Y these research practices were at most supplementary to the savvy characterization of a homoerotic poetic tradition in a language having critical currency. If one performed a discussion of literary history with a hip critical script, it seemed, the burdens of documentation, verification, and proof vanished.

So how was I supposed to respond to this paper? I had no desire to humiliate an earnest beginner, however offended I was by his submission. Besides, I did not interpret him as an incompetent undergraduate neglecting basic scholarly methods and values. Rather, I saw him as a clever neophyte imitating his superiors and learning the trade. This was obviously an intelligent and enterprising student who should have been directed toward reading major texts of literature, history, and philosophy and toward studying foreign languages. "Do a few years of homework before jumping into the professional fray," someone should have said to him. Unfortunately, he had been shown another avenue of advancement, one with shorter prep time and greater narcissistic satisfactions.

Given Y's frank indifference to research methods, where did he locate his paper's status as serious criticism? The assertions were unproven, so what gave them legitimacy? Obviously, their content. Y could forgo proof because his contentions carried a benevolent message: the recognition of homoerotic literature. His statements did not just sound good, they imported a moral good. Method did not matter because Y had fulfilled the primary aim of criticism announced by Professor X: to represent something deserving representation. Y's paper provided representation for heretofore repressed homosexual ideas and expressions and that acknowledgment overrode other methodological necessities. The thesis may have been vague, the logic loose, the evidence thin, but so long as Y brought homoerotic themes into the scholarly discussion, Y had performed an academic public service. To apply methodological objections to the representation would miss the point.

I then realized that I had nothing to say, no response to make. Customarily, my initial judgment of a piece of scholarship rested upon the consistency of its terms, the clarity of its ideas, the validity of its inferences. In disciplinary contexts, the social value and moral justice of its representations remained momentarily suspended. But Y did not inhabit that context and never would, so what would a methodological correction mean to him? This was a different language game, with different rules and admissions. To ask Y for a methodological clarification would be like handing a baseball to a quarterback in the middle of a football game. Y's gamebook began not with research principles but with certain represented contents. Professor X had announced a program for academics—to deliver social truths—and Student Y joined the program and reaped its rewards. To put it another way, Professor X's new disciplinary axiom had opened a professional niche in which a college junior with little knowledge and less competence could outline a methodologically disastrous but socially correct and morally indisputable representation and those individuals still relying on the old research criteria could do nothing to question it.

These two stories about representation provide a model of current critical praxis. Professor X's definition of academic labor and Student Y's performance of it condense the practice of literary study today into a neat formula: make represented content displace disciplinary methods as the standard of value. While methods submit sociohistorical content to institutional formalities and disciplines accommodate only the content that reflects disciplines' concerns, representation spurns all academic conventions and reveals the world's actual content (or at least claims to do so). While organized institutional inquiry operates through inbred codes and regularized procedures, representation maintains its fidelity to culture by following consistently no disciplinary codes or procedures, by eschewing precise definitions and strict research contingencies. In a word, representation criticism connects to the world by developing a strategically anti-disciplinary practice.

The bulk of this book is a terminological index of this disciplinary suicide. Because it details contemporary critical practice through an analysis of terms, call it a lexical autopsy of literary criticism. It is also a glossary of pathological terms, and a handbook of counterdisciplinary usage. While exposing the terminological usages as illogical, unsound, or inconsistent, the following glosses also seek to clarify them, to explain their methodological problems as strategic gestures, not as careless errors. Hence the following discussion may also constitute, though involuntarily, a primer of representational criticism, offering veteran and fledgling inquirers a lexical roadmap of anti-methodological pragmatics.

My thanks to Josué Harari, Marc Gotlieb, and Ralph Schoolcraft for their help in the conception and completion of this book. Grateful acknowledgment is made to Emory College and the Graduate School of Arts and Sciences for assistance in the publication of this book.

Introduction

To many professors of literature and language, overstepping the traditional boundaries of literary criticism seems like a good idea. It is good to expand criticism beyond the limits a purely aesthetic approach to literature entails. A commitment to literature as and only as literary art, to writings only in terms of their literary features, forces narrow, provincial, and elitist constraints upon our research and teaching. Clearly, when critics abstract literature from its historical, social, political, and institutional contexts, they falsify literature's reality. When academics divorce art from the world from which it originates, when formalists and theorists objectify a poem or prose work into an isolated piece of language, when humanists distinguish literature as an ethical whole transcending the material aspects of culture and society, they impoverish literature's significance and value. Even when they claim for literature a special ontological status such as universality, critics anaesthetize literature's political causes and social import. To counteract such spurious isolations and return literature to the truth of its actual existence, we must widen our inquiries, bring more historical variables and cultural contexts to bear upon our professorial work. By broadening our focus, we situate literature in a comprehensive sociohistorical matrix, our scholarly field now being culture at large.

So goes the prevailing wisdom in criticism today. Its call is simple, but pervasive: put literature back into its cultural context and convert textual analysis into cultural criticism. Influential books like Raymond Williams's *The Country and the City*, Edward Said's *The World, the Text, the Critic*, Frank Lentricchia's *Criticism and Social Change*, Jim Merod's *The Political Responsibility of the Critic*, Robert Scholes's *Textual Power*, John Brenkman's *Culture and Domination*,

Terry Eagleton's *Literary Theory: An Introduction*, and many others similarly inclined have successfully argued the political need and moral propriety of restoring literature to its cultural locus and beginning the job of historical reconstruction and critical intervention. For long enough, these critics say, conservative attitudes and bad faith have removed literature from its worldly involvements and made criticism into an impotent division of intellectual labor, secluded behind academic walls. Armed with the anti-formalist indictments by Karl Marx, Antonio Gramsci, Michel Foucault, Clifford Geertz, and other prestigious sponsors, these critics restore to literary texts their worldliness, their immersion in the actualities of social processes, institutions, capital, and power. Critics' hortatory pronouncements about the rightness of reconnecting literature to the world sound irrefutable. The premise they work on is seemingly self-evident: literature is a real cultural artifact, arising at a particular time and place, contingent on material and ideological conditions. Criticism that is authentic and true attends to those contingencies.

However, notwithstanding the insistent tone of these axioms, they contain a logical flaw. The problem: they use literary criticism's own subject matter, literature, to assert that the discipline fails rightly to understand and appreciate it. They take a disciplinary object ("literature"), a focus of study shaped and selected by the discipline itself, and then censure the discipline for misrepresenting that object. World-oriented critics chastise traditional literary criticism for inaccurately criticizing literature. But how can literary criticism misconceive the reality of literature when literary criticism has defined literature? As a disciplinary object, literature is a function of disciplinary definitions and methods, not a real thing preceding the disciplinary labor and occupying the world. Literary criticism proposes a concept of literature and gives literary language definitive attributes, and this is not a representation of literature, but a definition of it, and a definition cannot be a misrepresentation. It may be faulty, but not inaccurate. A definition may be rejected on pragmatic or institutional grounds, as when one school of criticism attacks another's definition of literature because it produces a failed pedagogy, but a definition cannot misconstrue the reality of what it defines. The only way a misrepresentation objection can stand up is if we deny the definitional aspect of criticism, that is, if we maintain the assumption that the literature the discipline refers to lies outside the academic teaching and scholarship of it. The argument that literary criticism falsifies literature holds only if literary criticism's literature stands apart from the discipline that researches it.

Now, of course, common sense says that literature exists outside literature departments. However, precise definitions of literature, definitions that provide for more than arrangements of bookstore shelves, that classify some writings as literary and others as non-literary, that give directions to scholarly inquiry and the training of students—these do not come before literature departments' institutional work. These are not popular and common sense definitions of literature, but rather specialized definitions that create disciplinary boundaries and academic departments and help practitioners administer an inquiry. The latter effectively occur only in disciplinary contexts, which could not do without them. The former, extradisciplinary understandings of literature (for example, literature is fiction, is verse form, is emotional expression) proceed everywhere else and do so haphazardly. This is not to say that popular conceptions of literature are wrong, but only that they do not give scholars much help in organizing a discipline of literary study. If one tried to base a literary study on a popular conception, the only knowledge one would produce is a popular knowledge—how to consume literature, how to find a novel in a bookstore or a poem in the library, how to distinguish fiction from non-fiction, plot from theme.

But a more than popular understanding of literature, an expertise in literary scholarship, requires greater learning, sharper distinctions, higher standards. Studying literature, analyzing and classifying and periodizing it, teaching scholars and students to turn their reading into a systematic practice, all call for a more rigorous definition of literature and a more sophisticated method of understanding it. If the study is to be organized and coherent, if it is to become a discipline, then it must begin by isolating a discrete subject matter and adopting a discrete method that focuses on that subject matter as such. Literary inquirers need to delimit some elements in the world into a class of literary objects accessible to critical inquiry, compose them into a scholarly field separate from other fields, the separation resting on a literary property that all objects within the field possess and all objects without it do not. On this model, the objects of the discipline of English literary criticism are made up of texts written originally in English and bearing the property of literariness (whatever that may be stipulated as). If we judge that limitation worthwhile, we then develop methods that operate precisely on the distinguishing properties, that preserve the field, that maintain the focus of the discipline as the methods are applied to individual instances of the class. In other words, a disciplinary inquiry into a subject like literature requires a definition of literature and a strategy that seeks out the literary, not the historical or the political or any other disciplinary creation. A discipline must have a method that yields correlative descriptions of the objects falling under the proposed definition. A disciplinary definition is given and a method follows that identifies those things that answer to the definition, and the discipline's success lies not so much in the truth of the definition as in the relative answerability of the method.

Given such method-oriented understandings, the judgment of a discipline's conception of its subject matter makes no sense if phrased only in terms of the conception's truth value, its correspondence to a real world object. The conception of literature by literary criticism is a definition, not a description, a stipulation, not a representation, and so to call it true or false mistakes its purpose. That purpose rests in the practical fact that the term plays first and foremost a methodological role in criticism. It is easy to interpret the phrase "literature is . . . " as an existential statement of what literature really *is*. But as a founding postulate of literary criticism, the phrase "literature is . . . " should be understood as "let 'literature' stand for. . . ." The definition should constitute an analytic statement of what we mean by the concept "literature," not an existential statement of what the object literature actually is. This is not to say that existential statements are wrong or illegitimate or impossible, but only that they are inappropriate to this formative disciplinary setting. In constructing a discipline within the Humanities, in mapping a subject and developing a method, we would like to say true things about the world, but inquirers' first ambition is to make the practice consistent, economical, pragmatic. If the goal is to organize an inquiry, we shift our priority from fidelity to reality to coherence of method. Then, we find that questions of the accuracy or correspondence of our conceptions of literature come after we determine how the conception fits in with a systematic method of interpretation. In the case of literary criticism, the definition of literature constitutes not an ontic description, but a methodological opening, the first step by which literary criticism differentiates itself from other forms of criticism.

So, the disciplinary definition of subject matter is a methodological act and is to be judged on methodological grounds, not on truth grounds. Some disciplines are formal, some are empirical. Some are historical, some are mathematical. Some require field work, some require laboratory work. Some work with written texts, some work with oral traditions. In all cases, what distinguishes the inquiries is not only the object of study but the approach to it. Even if we understand all cultural objects as texts, that does not mean their textuality is the same and remains the same through different methodological applications. The proof for this method criterion is that two disciplines can look at the same object and produce quite different, but not contradictory results. Literary criticism exists as a discrete discipline not only because it studies literature but also because it has a method that will do with a text something different from what another discipline will do with it. Furthermore, method here is not even strictly separate from its object, for the method is the very thing that spotlights literature and literary characteristics of language in the field of inquiry. The objectification of literature into literature is a literary method's initial proceeding.

This implies a pragmatic understanding of definitions and postulates. Statements like "literature is . . . " are on this basis instrumental, not representational. If disciplinary terms reach out to the world, they do so not by reflecting the world, but by making a portion of the world sensible, open to investigation. Their significance lies in their workability, their fitness for the interpretative work at hand. This is not to rule out their truth, but only to suspend it in favor of their usefulness to the inquiry. The justification for that suspension is a pragmatic one. Highlighting terms' utility instead of their truth, inquirers develop a consensual methodological language without raising too many difficult questions about the language's referential accuracy or ontological commitments. An examination of the method-language's fidelity to real things would interfere with its practical benefits, for that method-language makes inquiry economically communicable and reliably standardized because of the consistency of its terms, the serviceability of its postulates to certain desired results, not because of the groundedness of the language in real existences. It meets the institutional needs of a scholarly and pedagogic community, not the metaphysical needs of extra-inquiry truth seekers. And the language has not only an institutional sanction but a logical one by virtue of the following fact: if one wanted to determine whether the terms of inquiry denote things aright, one could do so, but then one would have to develop a new set of terms and methods with which to test them. But then, how is one to test those new terms' truth except by an examination with yet a newer set of terms, and then a newer . . . ?

Inquirers overcome that methodological impasse by postulating some basic ideas and predicates upon which to derive a field and a practice. The categories and abstractions they use to organize a discipline they do not find in the world. Rather, inquirers hypothesize and experiment with conceptual instruments until they fall into place as a systematic, reproducible interpretation. The fundamental tools are conceived and implemented, not found and followed, and so they retain the status of a conceptual apparatus, not extra-inquiry entities. A term like "literature" has several meanings, but as a focus of inquiry, that meaning is determined by its conventional use in literary critical methods. As a disciplinary invention, literature belongs to a conceptual framework that sets semantic limits upon it. The word means what it does in the framework's methods, the sentences the framework produces. The word's value rests mainly on how much it facilitates the inquiry's simplicity.

This is the response literary critics make to those who accuse them of depoliticizing, dehistoricizing, transcendentalizing, or otherwise misrepresenting literature. Literary critics focus on literary features at the expense of historical, political, and other worldly elements of the text not because they deny the latters' truth or significance. They study literariness because they consider it a worthwhile object of study. Literature is a field of inquiry, not a segment of reality or a slice of history. Literary criticism as a literary explication does not propose to unveil literature's historical existence. Instead, it fabricates a method of textual analysis, and its literary subject matter comes from a set of stipulated attributes, not from the world.

But does a pragmatic justification for literary criticism carry any weight in today's critical climate? None whatsoever. Indeed, the methodological rejoinder to the charge that literary criticism falsifies literature's reality many contemporary critics would say is precisely the point. Methodological defenses do not refute the falsification charge, but only confirm it. Cultural critics, historicists, and interdisciplinary scholars argue, the very problem with literary criticism is that it is methodologically grounded, not reality based. Method is too formal and too academically conditioned to remain true to social actualities. Pragmatic criteria are too insular, too self-referential to reach beyond their own self-sustaining professionalized norms. Put another way, the understanding of literature as a conceptual instrument, not a piece of concrete social reality, is a reification, one serving professional interests. Literature as a disciplinary invention, not a representation, converts a social object constructed by historical and material processes into a categorical term. As a conceptual component of the method of literary criticism, literature arises by abstraction, which is to say, by elimination of many actual interrelations literature has with the economics of book publishing, the politics of imperialism, the rise of domesticity, and other cultural and historical phenomena. Literary critics may, perhaps, admit to the abstraction and then point to the advantages of it, the coherence and stability that the isolation of literature from culture provides for literary study. Those practical benefits claimed for a pragmatic understanding of literature cultural and historicist critics also acknowledge—and condemn. To critics such as Bruce Robbins, Henry Giroux, Andrew Ross, and Stephen Greenblatt, the organization of inquiry into disciplines and specialties, a division carried out in part by the relation of terms to conceptual frameworks, not to cultural verities, submits the materials of history and society to institutional demands. (Greenblatt writes in *Learning to Curse*, "I wanted in fact to erase all boundaries separating cultural studies into narrowly specialized departments," 4.) Academic organization compartmentalizes knowledge and knowers into fields and experts, a workplace pigeonholing that mismanages historical truth.

Such demarcations and appropriations break up reality into artificial pieces and obscure the involvements literature has with politics, economics, ideology, racism, and repression. They disguise the dirty facts of capitalism and imperialism. In defining literature as *x*, literary criticism excludes *y*, *z*, and all the other items that *x* implicitly relates to, thereby repeating the same vicious exclusions operating in social and political life. Getting back to the truth of literature's real existence, then, compensates for all the institutional pressures to contain literary study within the comfortable limits of a formalized inquiry. Representing literature faithfully breaks the institutional proprieties of criticism, explodes the conceptual framework that keeps literary study apart from social affairs. Applied only to abstract objects conceived by definition, criticism is merely a skill, a facility in performing a disciplinary procedure. But applied to real objects observed in cultural contexts, criticism becomes an activist endeavor. Method entails a social withdrawal, while representation constitutes social intervention. The method of literary criticism must, therefore, give way to the accurate representation of literature, the real thing. This truth-criterion marks the way for literary criticism to return literature to culture, to expand analysis beyond purely literary concerns, to rescue critics from their disciplinary myopia and enroll them among the forces for social change.

This implies a realist conception of literary criticism. It is opposed to a pragmatic conception of critical inquiry in that a pragmatic approach concentrates on building a set of investigative habits and conventions that fulfill this or that inquiry's specific purpose, while a realist approach honors such habits only so long as they facilitate the one abiding purpose: representation of culture and society. Pragmatic methods promote the coherence of an intellectual practice. Realist methods proceed from a commitment to truth and justice in the real world. Though it often suggests a relativistic adjustment of beliefs and actions to expedience, "pragmatism" here signifies a stricter process: regularizing an orderly, consensus-based study of a field of objects. It diverges from realism in its primary concern for disciplinary integrity, not representational accuracy. This is why pragmatism is linked to disciplinary conduct (defining terms, giving postulates, outlining methods), realism (so defined) to extradisciplinary facts. The pragmatist assembles an order of concepts and observations, the realist yearns for the order of nature.

This is not to say that the latter actually does yield historical fact. Usually, realist critics express their representation objective only as a moral sanction, not a method, an injunction, not a practice. Under realist imperatives, criticism studies literature as it really is and the closer the interpretation corresponds to the work's reality, the better the criticism—a vague, but powerful principle. Though it does not specify what the reality is and how to get to it, the realist idea has a definitive effect. It undermines the conventions of inquiry, the terms, methods, and institutions of interpretation. Because the world pre-exists those conventions, implementing disciplinary conventions distorts the object, raises methodological prerequisites, rules of inquiry, and norms of evaluation above the object's existential condition. So, the less critical methods abstract the object from its real world interrelations, the more criticism succeeds. The more criticism neutralizes its own methodological contrivances, the less it reshapes literature into institutional images. The only significant evaluative question of criticism is, does it preserve the truth of what it studies?

One wonders, however, how a criticism based on the truth-criterion "correspondence to history and society" can function as a systematic, transmissible inquiry. If standardized method undermines the truth requirement, how is representational criticism supposed to proceed? How can critics make their inquiry correspond to the object's extra-inquiry reality? To make criticism adequate to literature's reality, criticism would have to be as varied and fluid as that reality. How coherent and effective would such an activity be when it came time to ask students to learn and reproduce it, colleagues to assess it, administrators to administer it? If we lift institutional and methodological restraints on literary study, if we do not circumscribe the object within a formal definition of literature and a method of literary analysis that pursues only what falls under that definition, then we enlarge the domain of literary study to include politics, history, and society. In doing so, we move closer to more accurate representations of the whole literary object.

But also, as we draw more and more contextual material into textual analysis, we sacrifice uniformity in the practice of criticism. A wholesale introduction of historical content into the conception of literature may satisfy a correspondence conception of inquiry, but it also causes disorganization in the enterprise. With so many realities to choose from—political, social, personal, scientific, linguistic, and so on—scholars and teachers have no clear way of scaling scholarship and teaching down to workable proportions. If the truth about literature demands that we involve society, history, politics, experience in the understanding of literature, one might ask what is the method that enables us to do so? If method itself slides into suspect institutional and narrow disciplinary forms, what shape can criticism assume? What principle of accumulation will make the plurality of political, historical, and sociological interpretations more than an aggregate of interpretations talking about different things—a political reading highlighting political elements in the object, a sociological reading highlighting sociological elements in the object, . . . ?

In sum: how can representational criticism become a common practice when the means of reproduction and standardization—regular methods, consensus norms, instrumental concepts—appropriate the historical truth representational criticism seeks to honor? If critics' commitment to historical truth compels them to regard disciplinary structures as enervating the representation of and participation in social change, how can critics establish that commitment as a widespread principle without using the very kinds of institutionalization they disdain? In deciding the conflict between true representation and conventional method, in decrying disciplinary coherence in the name of social engagement, critics face a circumstantial impasse: how to make representational criticism into a sanctioned practice. For the establishment of representation as a viable critical practice carries with it a set of practical exigencies that are themselves not representational, but methodological. These include: what pedagogy best serves representational training? What language best suits it? What standards of evaluation distinguish a good representation from a bad one? Such questions about training, terminology, and evaluation follow not from realist demands, but from pragmatic pressures. As soon as inquirers begin to ask "how do we teach representation? how do we rank representations? how do we verify them?" they begin to turn away from represented content and develop protocols of inquiry, manners of presentation, standards of clarity, and other methodological criteria.

This necessity of not only making representations but of handling them, teaching them, evaluating them, in a word, institutionalizing them, causes representation critics an annoying ambivalence. Representation tugs at their social instincts and moral scruples, while method serves their teaching and administrative duties, their scholarly judgment, and their desire to popularize their practice. The conflict between correct representation and systematic inquiry seems unresolvable. However, representational criticism has developed, of late, a solution to it: a practice that works against method. Contemporary criticism strives to represent literature and the culture it springs from as they really happen and so it treats the terms and procedures of the representation as threatening abstractions. For the content of the representation to be true, then, the forms of the representation must be minimized or canceled. As criticism pulls literature out of the world and into its interpretative field, criticism must ward off any institutional designs and disciplinary constraints that expel literature's worldly traits and affiliations. It must protect historical truth from methodological takeovers. The language and gestures of criticism must remain representational, not pragmatic. Critical practice must not slip into mechanical rituals of discipline. It must not let its terms become customary tools, methodological signposts.

This means that the language of literary-cultural interpretation must operate in a curiously ambivalent way. The terms of criticism must advance the interpretation and do so recognizably, for the interpretation must qualify as representational criticism and a conventional idiom is one of the forms of qualification. But those terms must not settle into an orthodox parlance. So, critics implement such terms as necessary to identify the representational activity, but then annul the methodological and disciplinary goals that normally go along with those terms. Representational criticism invokes critical terms that imply a methodological proceeding, but then abandons the follow-up parts of the inquiry, the clarification of the terms, the logical and empirical implementation of them. This is the strategy of representational criticism: to introduce critical terms, yet withhold the methods that substantiate them.

Let us elucidate that rather elliptical formulation of representational practice with an example. The first sentence of Homi Babha's *The Location of Culture* runs: "It is the trope of our time to locate the question of culture in the realm of the *beyond.*" This is a curious sentence. It says that there is such a thing as "*the* trope of our time" and "*the* question of culture" and "*the* realm of *the* beyond." The definite articles signal a proclamation: out of all the tropes of our time, here is *the* trope; out of all the questions one could ask about or of culture, here is *the* question; out of all the beyonds one could locate the question of culture in, Babha locates it in the very realm of the beyond per se. Presumably, the remainder of the chapter will specify this trope, this question, and this beyond and clarify these inflated judgments.

But before we proceed to follow Babha's exposition, we still note something odd about Babha's sentence: "It is the trope of our time to locate the question of culture in the realm of the *beyond*." The proposition has a subject and a predicate, respectively, the trope and the location. That is, this trope is a particular action. Babha's grammar makes something normally defined as a figure of speech into the locating of a question. But how can the placement of a cultural question in the beyond be itself a trope? The OED defines "trope" variously as a "figure of speech which consists in the use of a word or phrase in a sense other than that which is proper to it"; as "an embellishment into some part of the text of the mass [of the Western Church]"; or as the "reciprocal of a node on a curve or surface." The only OED meaning remotely similar to Babha's is the trope of ancient skepticism, that being a logical procedure for refuting dogmatism, but this can hardly be Babha's intention. *The New Princeton Encyclopedia of Poetry and Poetics* defines "trope" as, along with "figure" and "scheme," "parts of what is collectively called rhetorical or 'figurative' language." The entry then goes on to discuss the distinction between "proper" meanings and "divergent" meanings and then distinguishes different types of tropes from one another—a discussion in no way touching Babha's usage. Finally, the major contemporary theorist of tropes, Paul de Man, characterizes "trope" as all the figures of speech conventionally understood as such. Of course, de Man seeks to undo the relation between figural and literal, to show that "trope is not a derived, marginal, or aberrant form of language but the linguistic paradigm par excellence" (*Allegories of Reading*, 105). However, though de Man asserts that metaphor, metonymy, and so on are in a way more fundamental and originary than literal words, he still treats trope as a verbal structure. Not one of his examples extends "trope" to non-linguistic actions, as Babha does. According to all these definitions of trope, one may use tropes in speech, but one may make the use itself into a trope only by making it part of another verbal use, by verbalizing it in tropic ways.

There is no precedent for Babha's usage simply because it does not make sense to call an act of locating a question somewhere a "trope." The word "beyond" may be a trope, as may be "our time" and "the question of culture." How these words may function as metaphors, metonymies, ironies, or whatever remains unclear, but the possibility exists. But if I say, "Let us pose the question of culture tomorrow" or " . . . beyond the classroom," though I may have uttered a trope, the utterance itself is not a trope. My statement may have an allegorical significance of some kind or my words may have a metaphorical or ironic import, but the act of stating them does not. I can describe the act metaphorically, but I cannot make the act itself a metaphor.

Such slippages of terminology do not amount to a creative use of critical tools. Rather, they indicate a conceptual fuzziness, a slack attention to concepts' meaning and purview. Although a rhetorical connection may be drawn between "trope" and "location," there is no logical or epistemological identity of "trope" and "location" (the identity suggested by Babha's statement). One cannot justify the trope-location assertion; indeed, Babha does not try to do so. Babha does not explore the conceptual structure of trope or map its relations to literal meaning or outline its implications for the interpretation of literature and language. Babha's usage merely confounds the clear sense of "trope." If one were to counter that Babha redefines "trope," then he has done so ineffectively. His redefinition does not clarify or improve upon the older meaning. For, if "trope" can refer to a verbal structure and to a non-verbal action such as choosing to locate a question in a beyond, then we have enlarged its extension to the point where it has no specificity and little explanatory value. If "trope" refers to both verbal and non-verbal acts, then the term applies so broadly that it adds little to any description of any act. What is the value of redefinition if it does not sharpen distinctions and enhance descriptions?

Technical words such as "trope" signify certain objects and imply certain interests and endeavors. When one uses the word "trope" in a scholarly context, one also invokes implicitly a contrast with literal meaning, a group of instances (metaphor, allegory, irony, etc.), a type of analysis (rhetorical and formalist criticism), and a set of theorists (Aristotle, Quintilian, Thomas Aquinas, Jacques Derrida, etc.). These implications amount to a methodological burden that reaches beyond the term's mere utterance. Once one mentions "trope" in a textual commentary, one introduces a strategic complication into any paraphrase of the text's content. Trope adds formal, nonrepresentational wrinkles to the commentary and to ignore them and simply treat the text literally is to interpret inconsistently. A method of analyzing tropes differs from a method of analyzing literal meaning. The concepts of meaning, reference, representation, and so on have different values in each sphere. If a critic casually asserts that the text has a significant tropic dimension, then standards of validity call for a consistent, pertinent, and satisfactory description of those tropes (as trope) and how they work. The assumption of language as literal representation must be provisionally suspended.

This is to say that, as a rule, "trope" and other operative critical terms commit users of them to whatever concepts and methods are implied by the terms. The most important terms in any discipline carry within themselves necessary dispositions. When critics implement a critical term in a scholarly context, they dispose themselves to accounting consistently for related terms and oppositions and to substantiating the implementation with an appropriate method. The use of some concepts disallows the use of some others. Some assertions require one kind of evidence, other assertions require quite another kind of evidence. A formal analysis of Alexander Pope's heroic couplet reveals much about his metrical technique, but it says nothing about the Court of George II. However, a historical analysis of Pope's heroic couplet (what other poets said about it, what kinds of poems it was customarily used in, what subject matters it fit, what readers inferred from it, etc.) can turn Pope's couplet into some form of historical evidence. The thing to do is to determine what kind of historiographical purposes the couplet-evidence serves, what conclusions one can draw from it, what concepts apply to it.

However, this type of methodological coherence works against the representational goals of criticism. "Trope" and its methodological burdens abide by pragmatic criteria of consistency and coherence, not truth criteria of representational accuracy. So why does Babha use "trope," a technical term calling for an acknowledged method of analysis? Certainly not to signal a rhetorical explication, as would normally be the case. Rather, the word "trope" and its subsequent neglect, its lack of methodological substantiation, satisfies the ambivalent goals of representational criticism. Babha's usage of "trope" effectively straddles the line between professional skill and cultural involvement. The term is technical enough to certify Babha's expertise, yet it is vague enough to prevent his expertise from being slotted into a neat disciplinary category like "scholar of rhetoric." The word grants him intellectual status, but its hazy application to "our time" keeps his intellectuality from becoming academic. Combining "trope" with "culture," Babha provides a description of culture in a language satisfying his need for authority, yet stopping short of authorizing him as merely an academic inquirer carrying out this or that disciplinary job. If Babha proceeded to delineate the tropic nature of various acts of culture-location, he would stop talking about culture and instead concentrate on a rhetorical structure. He would become a specialist in figurative language, not a culture watcher. The mere mention of "trope" sets him apart from unskilled observers, but the absence of method keeps his skillfulness from being too professionalized. We have a jargon term offered as colloquial and an implicit insight whose lack of supporting evidence and premises shelters it from disciplinarity.

This is a strategic obscurantism. The strategy is to use disciplinary terms like "trope" but then neglect the method that goes with them, thereby saving ourselves and our subject matter from disciplinary cooptation. Critics cite the terms and profit from their official connotations, but they resist obeying the methods that go with them, and do so to retain their fidelity to the object and their freedom from institutions.

This is the anti-method of representational criticism. Such a novel practice calls for a new glossary, one that lays out representational criticism's terminology and usage. The equivocations of representational criticism are subtle and complex, and unless one diagnoses its usages as the outcome of a pragmatic-representational opposition, much contemporary criticism will strike readers as confused, incoherent, or nonsensical. The following mini-essays on critical terms are designed to lift that incomprehension, to rationalize the confusions as natural consequences of criticism's anti-method proceedings. The intent is clarification. If the result should be a critique, I leave its consequences for my readers to draw.

A Critical Glossary

List of Terms Included

construction
cultural poetics
cultural studies
decisive assertions
deconstruction
discipline
discourse
essentialize
gender
ideology
-ing
interdisciplinary

literary criticism
the logic of
political criticism
problematize
the question of
radical
rethink
sociology of literature
theory
voice
what so-and-so calls

construction   The word "construction" has become so popular in contemporary criticism that its mention and reception are almost as routine as those of terms like "irony" and "plot." The MLA Bibliography lists 2,861 entries for the word since 1981, and titles bearing the heading "The Construction of . . . " litter journal tables of contents, conference banners, and academic press catalogues. Typical examples are "Communication and the Construction of Homosexuality," "The Construction of Consumer Desire in the Twenties," "Shakespeare's English History Plays and the Construction of the Gendered Subject," "Primetime Television and the Construction of Postfeminism," and "Emerson, Liberalism, and the Construction of Nationality." These and other instances of constructivist criticism reveal how extensively and customarily the term "construction" now reaches into different historical, literary,

political, psychoanalytical, and textual realms. What the prolifera-
tion and diversity of constructivist critical practices indicates is a
general attitude spanning the critics' subject matters and lying at
the root of the commentaries. This fundamental principle, the
constructivist position, motivates a large and otherwise dissimilar
group of practitioners from different fields with disparate interests
to apply constructivist analysis to manifold aspects of culture and
history. Clearly, as the titles above show, the objects of constructivist analysis may range from epistemological entities like the self
to basic concepts like the aesthetic to historical periods like modernism to a variety of other phenomena.

One abiding purpose for constructivist inquiry is to assert the
constructivist premise, namely, that x IS a construction. That is,
the use of "the construction of x" formula marks an insistent
denial of any extra-human, extra-historical basis for x. God, Nature,
Essence, Spirit, Fate—such metaphysical agents have no active role
in the genesis and structure of x and are, in fact, themselves constructs. In constructivist thinking, in the production of human reality, life, and culture, metaphysical and transhistorical constants
give way to politics, society, ideology, interest, and desire. Enlight-
ened individual will is not included, though; it smacks too much
of transcendence or humanism to qualify as a construction worker.
Anything in the human world, which is the only world we have, has a
human origin (whether because of human creativity or human me-
diation makes no difference). To believe otherwise is to subscribe to
naïveté, nostalgia, bad faith, false consciousness, and so on. Construction criticism contests those metaphysical illusions and over-
turns all the spurious apologetics designed to bolster them. Tracing
x's development back through its cultural circulations and historical permutations, lifting its ideological disguises and wrecking its
metaphysical justifications, constructivist criticism reveals the actual sociohistorical grounds and goals of x's existence.

Accepting on faith the axiom "Everything is a construction of
some sort," construction criticism does not bother with any logical
and ontological quarrels with the constructivist attitude. With a basic principle in hand, inquiry involves merely the discrimination of
constructions. Constructivist critics carry out the task of explaining
the nature of this or that construction and the value of their explanation depends upon the specificity, detail, and documentation of
the descriptions they devise. For, if everything is a construction,

then the mere assertion that x is a construction is a useless tru-
ism. Unless we can distinguish the construction of x from that of y
and z, our inquiry lapses into constructivist platitudes and begs the
question of how, why, when, and by what or whom x is actually
constructed.

This method of discrimination, largely a historical description, is
what the term "construction" calls for. However, scholars do not
often develop scrupulous and thorough accounts of x's construction. For accurately recounting the construction of x places massive
historiographical burdens upon researchers. The phrase "the construction of x" names a formidably complex process and the reconstruction of that construction requires copious evidence, empirical
support, meticulous documentation from a variety of sources and
domains. In recognizing x as a social construct, we acknowledge
that x is determined by innumerable historical, political, textual,
physical, and other variables. To formulate all these elements into
a coherent and correct rendition of x's construction, critics must
gather large amounts of historical information, assemble the pertinent facts, examine the constitutive propositions, itemize the
prevailing social relations, interpret the relevant texts, and then
organize all that material along the lines of the constructivist ontology of sociohistorical processes.

We can see how difficult and laborious such research is as soon
as we begin to address a particular topic. Say x signifies "masculine
identity in Victorian England." What questions must we answer if
we propose to outline the construction of masculine identity in Victorian England? First, we have to establish some historical parameters. Does "masculine identity" refer to the same thing in London
as in the Welsh countryside? Does it mean in 1842 the same thing
it means in 1882? Does it represent the same thing on the battle-
field as it does in the university or in the church? Does it circulate
in texts like Gothic novels the same way it does in Birmingham fac-
tories or in ballrooms in Bath? In other words, we must not lazily
presume that the phrase "masculine identity in Victorian England"
sufficiently pins down our subject to a manageable semantic compass. The phrase perhaps denotes in the abstract a single concept, but as soon as we try to place it historically and begin our
construction analysis, we discover a multitude of diverse references
and connotations. In that case, without any further specifications,
"masculine identity in Victorian England" simply has too many

historical meanings for one inquiry to handle it properly. This is not to say that every historical topic must have only a single reference. However, pragmatically speaking, beyond a certain semantic point, inquirers must fix some contextual boundaries for the topic, the boundaries being set at the places where the meaning of "masculine identity in Victorian England" changes significantly enough to warrant recontextualization. Within those boundaries, the term may still have variations of meaning and reference, but those variations may be adequately accounted for by historical data and textual evidence.

Having set geographical and chronological limits to the analysis of "masculine identity in Victorian England," we reduce our subject matter's semantic complexities to workable levels. But now comes the hard part: to delineate all the things that went into the construction of the subject matter. For, even in its narrowed context, say, aristocratic London society from 1850 to 1870, "masculine identity" still emerges from an intricate mixture of sources and causes. Some possibilities to consider: the Crimean War, legal statutes, Carlyle's hero worship and Mill's liberalism, evolution, the Women's Rights movement, Heathcliff, Queen Victoria and Prince Albert, colonial pursuits in Africa, Arnold's *Poems* (1853), Spencer's *The Principles of Psychology* (1855), and *Punch* cartoons. Only an exhaustive historical method of profuse citation and detailed analysis of texts ranging from daily newspapers to academic treatises and events ranging from the rise of Napoleon III to the marriage of the Brownings and settings ranging from the chambers of Parliament to the Chelsea breakfast table can begin to account for these and all the other ingredients of Victorian masculine identity. To produce an accurate reconstruction of that identity in all its historical richness and heterogeneity, to approximate its evolving social meanings and successive cultural manifestations, inquirers must compose thorough catalogues of empirical data and careful interpretations of complex phenomena. If construction is a historical process, then we must follow that process by admitting as many significant historical variables as we can into the reconstruction.

However, if constructivist inquirers effectively cope with the difficulties of comprehending and recounting the past by covering the relevant range of historical causes and contexts, their catholic approach raises yet another methodological problem. In fulfilling historiographical requirements in this manner, they face a new impasse, this time not an historical one, but a conceptual one. As critics move from one historical factor in the construction of x to another, they find that x itself changes. If they broach Victorian masculine identity by highlighting the example of Prince Albert, Chinese Gordon, Sir Richard Burton, and other famous agents of the British Empire, then critics conceive masculine identity as a sociopolitical icon, a public image. If they study masculine identity by listing statutes and legal decisions regarding citizenship, property rights, voting rights, connubial rights, inheritance laws, and so on, then critics treat masculine identity as a legal definition. If critics discuss it by reproducing popular and artistic representations of the male body, then critics set forth masculine identity as a physical structure. If they study masculine identity by describing behavior in certain domestic or political situations, then they conceive it as a particular form of domestic or political conduct. If critics then analyze that conduct psychologically or psychoanalytically, they thereby refer that conduct to a psychic structure, not a domestic or political one, and reconceive masculine identity as a psychic condition.

We could multiply such instances of different categorical versions of masculine identity and coordinate with each one a proper analytical technique. We must remember, however, that in each case we have not a construction of Victorian masculine identity per se, but the construction of Victorian masculine identity as an image construct, a legal construct, a physical construct, a behavioral construct, or a psychic construct. In focusing on different manifestations of masculine identity, we conceive masculine identity differently, this because of the methodological principle that says the choice of certain materials as evidence of x shapes retroactively the nature of x. For example, if we choose to explore masculine identity by looking at visual images of it, we do not thereby determine masculine identity per se, but only masculine identity as a visual image. The selection of one class of objects as illustrations of x automatically classifies x, narrows it to the predicates common to all the objects within the class. In jumping from one class to another, say, in switching from visual images of the male body to legal codes regarding men's rights, critics substitute both raw materials and the concept, meaning, abstraction, or truth the materials materialize.

This hermeneutical change is a methodological effect that construction usage wishes to ignore. This is where the absence of method proves advantageous, why the lack of conceptual specification is strategic. Constructivism implies that legal, physical, psychological, and other versions are really parts of one general construction of one thing, Victorian masculine identity. The critical question then becomes how to arrange them together, how to replicate the historical process that aligned them all into a prevailing, more or less unified cultural meaning. But in subdividing masculine identity into a series of subconstructs, inquirers break up the holistic reality of masculine identity. As soon as critics narrow the masculine construction's historical parameters and conceive masculinity in some categorical way (legally, familially, etc.), critics separate masculinity into disciplinary pieces. By chopping off one historical context and taking one perspective upon it, scholars compartmentalize constructivist inquiry into institutionally congenial subsets. Art historians look at images, literary critics look at novels, psychologists look at family roles, and so on. Victorian masculinity gets reproduced in the academy as arbitrary bits of disciplinary study—a falsification of masculinity's crossdisciplinary existence.

To avoid that appropriation, constructivists follow the citation-nonmethod pattern. They cite the word "construction" to make contact with historical process. They hold off from delimiting the construction historically and conceptually to maintain their fidelity to the construction's complexity and heterogeneity. For example, in the Introduction to two issues of *Cultural Critique* devoted to "The Construction of Gender and Modes of Social Division," editors Donna Przybylowicz, Nancy Hartsock, and Pamela McCallum say of the volumes' essays, "these readings and analyses take as their point of departure the construction of gender within an objective situation whose constraints may be psychological-familial, socio-economic, or cultural" (9). One expects that the essays will focus on an "objective situation" and detail its empirical and discursive particulars. And yet not a single essay addresses such a situation for more than a page or two. If we consider a text an "objective situation," then three essays consistently discuss gender issues in them (Jane Marcus on *Nightwood*, McCallum on Carlyle's *The French Revolution*, and Sydney Bryn Austin on media coverage of AIDS and Africa). However, as textual analyses, even these pieces fail to reach an "archaeology or excavation of certain sites of knowledge

[that] would place intellectual issues within specific sociopolitical situations" (10). The contributors broach gender within the provenance of discursive generalities like "The Gender of Critical Theory," "Feminism, Postmodernism, and the Critique of Modernity," and "Gender Hegemonies." The specific sociopolitical situations are only distantly gestured at, highlighted at the start but remaining a deferred end. The construction method persists as a theoretical circling around sociopolitical realities.

It is important to read the absence of documentation and clarification, the insistence on generality, not simply as a matter of laziness or incompetence. It is a principle of true representation. Diverse causes go into a construction, and to pursue any one of them too rigorously or to isolate one of a construction's "objective situations" would be to render the inquiry partial, to slip into disciplinary habits. To delve too deeply into, say, popular Victorian images of masculinity would sequester inquirers from other aspects of masculinity. The objectivity of this or that situation reduces the construction of gender to too narrow limits. It freezes the processual nature of construction and yields a fractional thing—a misrepresentation of all the forces and perspectives that go into gender's construction. The farther inquirers pursue a particular line of interpretation, which is usually disciplinarily forged, the less they can unite it with other lines of interpretation and build up an accurate description of x as a multifaceted cultural construct. Though the inquiry must, therefore, remain general, withholding method honors a higher aim than precision: maintaining the real constructivist existence of the object. The fact that this principle of generality saves scholars time and trouble of research and argument is merely a fortuitous benefit.

cultural poetics   Associated mainly with the work of Stephen Greenblatt, who derives it from Clifford Geertz's "interpretive anthropology," the term "cultural poetics" does not itself appear often in contemporary criticism. But nevertheless, it embodies the prime impulse of many scholars today: to bring literary analysis to cultural critique. As an anthropologico-literary heading, "cultural poetics" is a mediating term, uniting heretofore disjoined fields of action—culture and poetics. Culture is a real world entity, hard to pin down but still historically existent, awaiting the anthropologist's empirical observations and political judgments. In studying culture, inquirers immerse themselves in it, experience directly its exchanges and consumptions. But poetics is an abstract system, hard to implement but easy to formulate, an object not of concrete empirical treatment but of aesthetic commentary. In studying poetics, critics learn a set of aesthetic concepts and analyze poetic structures. The cultural contexts of those concepts' and structures' origin and instantiation remain out of play.

Cultural poetics skillfully combines these two ostensibly opposed procedures. It draws poetics out of abstraction, puts poetics into social circulation, and it lifts culture out of pure materiality, reveals culture's semiotic aspect. Poetic form becomes anthropologized and cultural reality becomes textualized. Greenblatt neatly encapsulates this integrating function: "Ever since anthropologists began to speak of the cultures they study as textual, and literary critics began to speak of the texts they study as cultural, one of the dreams of cultural poetics has been to link the text of anthropology and the text of literary criticism" ("Eating of the Soul," 97). Note that neither text is reduced to the other, but rather that the two are "linked." Avoiding a social science or a humanities partiality, cultural poetics is not simply the social contextualization of art, nor is it merely the aesthetic analysis of cultural objects. Rather, cultural poetics explores the space traversed by each appropriation, the area across which culture and art (and anthropology and literary criticism) play tug of war. Cultural poetics works in this indeterminate space and not at the sociohistorical or formal ends of it because, as Geertz puts it in *Local Knowledge*, "art is neither some transcendent phenomenon variously disguised in different cultures nor a notion so thoroughly culture-bound as to be useless beyond Europe" (12). Art is neither universal nor cultural, if by "cultural" we mean "relevant only to a single culture." Art as universal rests upon a long-exploded notion of transcendence, while art as monocultural stems from the position that only ideas and values originating in a culture properly apply to that culture. (Geertz calls this "culturalism.") The compromise necessitated by each pole's unacceptability is that art is crosscultural and that cultural poetics studies both the cultural meanings of art and the transcultural forms of art.

That is, cultural poetics studies works of art in cultural contexts, but also examines the works' elements that are not reducible to a single cultural context. This negotiation between an artwork's specific cultural determinants and its capacity to transcend *those* determinants (not all determinants) requires of the critic a great deal of circumspection and balance. (Greenblatt calls Geertz an "intellectual equilibrist . . . with an exquisite sense of balance"—"Eating of the Soul," 97.) For, in carrying out a crosscultural analysis of art, cultural poetics critics risk asserting a historical or causal relation between cultures where none exists. To avoid that historiographical error, critics draw connections between one context or object and another but leave the connection in a speculative mode, historically or positivistically unsubstantiated. For example, for a brief moment in "Deep Play: Notes on the Balinese Cockfight" (in *The Interpretation of Cultures*), Geertz compares Balinese onlookers to Shakespeare's audience, but does nothing more than note the relation. Likewise, in *The Predicament of Culture*, James Clifford opens with an ethnographic analysis of a poem from William Carlos Williams's *Spring and All*, focusing on Williams's maid-helper Elsie. Then, after the transitional clause "Only one of Elsie's emergent possibilities, the one connected with her 'dash of Indian blood,' is explored in this book" (7), Clifford recounts a 1977 Boston trial in which descendents of Wampanoag Indians sued for lost lands and had first to prove their tribal identity. Obviously, Clifford sees some connection between Williams's Elsie and the Wampanoags, but he does not clarify what it is. Instead, he merely juxtaposes both situations. Finally, Greenblatt parallels in "The Eating of the Soul" New Guinea death rituals and Shakespearean death scenes, but he guards against inferring from the parallel anything more than a tenuous analogical linkage.

This is to say, cultural poetics marks out art's crosscultural significance by composing striking new arrangements of diverse cultural materials, arrangements not determined by historical or causal relations, but by the connection's interpretative payoff. As Greenblatt characterizes Geertz's comparison, "Balinese cockfighting and the Shakespearean spectacle of treachery and damnation . . . are made to touch and resonate" ("Eating of the Soul," 98). "Resonance" Greenblatt elsewhere defines as "the power of the object displayed to reach out beyond its formal boundaries to a larger world, to evoke in the viewer the complex, dynamic cultural forces from which it has emerged and for which as metaphor or more simply as metonymy it may be taken by a viewer to stand" (*Learning to Curse*, 170). Also, "Among the most resonant moments are those in which the supposedly contextual objects take on a life of their own, make a claim that rivals that of the object that is formally privileged" (172). Cultural poetics contrasts yield a resonance in "viewers" that both makes the contrasted objects serve as representations of their cultural context and grants to them a "life" beyond that context. The outcome is not an addition of anthropological data or a revision of literary interpretation, but rather a new experience of objects and cultures. An "evocation," a "resonance" takes place in the sensitized eye of the beholder. Cultural poetics produces not historical discoveries or poetic theories, but edifying insights. The "touch and resonance" renders "illuminating alternatives, instructive differences, visions of mutual estrangement" ("Eating of the Soul," 99). The crosscultural comparisons do not reveal common grounds of each culture, but instead unveil ideological and material phenomena unique to each culture. Only by contrast with something categorically similar to them but in its cultural specifics drastically dissimilar (as the spectacles of a cockfight and *Macbeth*) will a culture's contents rise up from the homogenous background of a familiar world and become fully delineated.

This estranging experience of culture is the upshot of cultural poetics and rationalizes the usage of its apparently oxymoronic title. Cultural poetics is cultural, but not quite historical, aesthetic, but not quite formalist. To represent culture, it draws analogies whose justification is epistemological, not logical or historical. It enhances one's experience of art, deepens one's awareness of cultural relativism, forestalls an ethnocentric attitude toward others. The analogies may have little basis in fact or form, but so long as they bring about the defamiliarizing cognition, they count as legitimate instances of cultural poetics inquiry.

Of course, many historians and anthropologists object to such arbitrary couplings, claiming that the experiential benefit of them does not outweigh their violation of historical truth. Greenblatt notes how new historicists (here the same as cultural poeticists) are often accused of "conjoin[ing] what should by rights be kept apart, gluing together in a zany collage pieces that do not properly belong in the same place" ("Eating of the Soul," 99). But such accusations are wrong-headed, for they invoke a historiographical standard that cultural poetics never intended to observe in the first place. Besides, Greenblatt asks, "how do we know what is 'proper'?

Who controls the categories that govern the distinction between the arbitrary and the appropriate?" (99).

Unenlightened critics might respond, "We do! We scholars and professors are the ones who determine what is proper. That is what we are trained to do and what our culture entrusts us to do." But such narrow institutional forms of governance rightly apply only to those practices working under them. A historian's judgments pertain to historical research whose aim is accurate reconstruction, not to cultural poetics research whose aim is collage and revelation. In light of cultural poetics' frankly analogical techniques, historiographical and logical criticisms of cultural poetics sound like illiberal exercises of institutional power, rearguard actions of disciplines jealously guarding their turf. The very term "cultural poetics" highlights this inappropriateness of the historical attack. In being a "poetics," the inquiry renounces any positive historical identity. Individual cultural poetics interpretations may imply directions for further historical study, but the assemblages of texts and contexts they fashion make no immediate historical claim. Of course, cultural poetics would never wish to contradict historical fact. But because history is best understood as a complex network of representations, social forces, and material contingencies that catches human beings up in "webs of significance" (Geertz's phrase), the cultural poetics scholar has ample semiotic room to play in beyond the established facts. That semiotic slippage, excess, liminality, in a word, "resonance," provides the critic with his or her raw materials. Hence the substitution of "cultural" for "historical." "History" carries too many materialist vestiges. But "culture" immediately introduces representation and simulacra into social reality. Furthermore, if inquiry approaches a cultural context as "a problem not in social mechanics but in social semantics," if it examines culture as "an assemblage of texts" (Geertz, *Interpretation of Cultures*, 448), then a poetics method will reveal more about culture than will a traditional historical method. The adjective "cultural" does not eliminate historical questions, but cultural poetics broaches historical reality only in so far as it makes creative use of historical materials. Again, cultural poetics proposes not primarily to reconstruct a cultural context, but rather to sharpen the perception of cultural differences.

This is the advantage of the term "cultural poetics." It impinges on historical truth, but it fends off historiographical standards. It appeals to the textual skills of literary scholars, but it escapes the formalism of literary criticism. It speaks of culture, but it transcends the limits of positivist social science. The term points to a method of suggestion, of illuminating cultural insights having as of yet unverified historical sanction. Within the space of cultural poetics, a space of representations and forces, not of concrete things and ideal forms, inquirers verge on historical fact but never settle there. Culture is a text, a dynamic symbolic construct whose workings constitute a "poetics of everyday behavior" (Greenblatt, *Learning to Curse*, 154), not an inert set of facts. So, the best approach to culture is not through an empirical catalogue of historical causes and events, but through a poetics of cultural processes. Finally, lest this poetics drift off into aesthetic abstraction, inquirers read the cultural text ever mindful of the text's historical contingencies. This is the methodological negotiation the term "cultural poetics" names.

But if the term "cultural poetics" steers between historical certainties and aesthetic judgments and discounts the full demonstration of either one, what vindicates cultural poetics as a serious inquiry? Two things: one, its moral outcome and, two, Geertz. The moral benefit of cultural poetics is that it inculcates a sensitivity to other cultures, specifically, a knowledge of other cultures that does not seek to eradicate those cultures' otherness. As readers follow c.p. critics on their excursions from one cultural context to another, readers begin to sense the strangeness of cultural difference. They witness not the timeless verities of human existence or the universal humanity underlying historical, geographical, and linguistic disparities, but rather the fundamental otherness of other peoples. As c.p. critics "try to understand cultures that seem disturbingly different from our own" (Greenblatt, "Eating of the Soul," 100), they allow that disturbance to happen. Cultural poetics understanding does not seek to assimilate other cultures to familiar ethical and epistemological categories. Rather, it accepts the other culture's disconcerting, seemingly unnatural nature and, most importantly, lets that unfamiliarity recoil back upon itself: "For the point of difference is not to secure the familiar but to render it too as strange, uncanny, wonderful" ("Eating of the Soul," 100).

In consequence of this defamiliarizing procedure, putatively natural behaviors have to be reinterpreted as conscious decisions, thoughtlessly held attitudes need to be rethought, and cultural arrogance must be abandoned. To recognize the other culture, to comprehend fully its signs and meanings and forms of life, inquirers must decenter their own signs and meanings. Cultural poetics linkages facilitate this cultural disengagement and its consequent receptivity. In sum, c.p. crosscultural analogies have a deprivileging effect. Neither the other cultures nor the inquirer's culture has a greater metaphysical claim to superiority, and this leveling of cultural prestige occasions a more imaginative, less selfish experience of the world. Cultural poetics is thus the antidote to cultural imperialism. Who would argue against this liberal conclusion? Who would place cultural poetics' methodological frailty above its ethical contribution?

This is not to say that cultural poetics has only a moral ground and not a methodological support. It does have the latter: Geertz. Geertz supplies literary scholars with a few pat and eminently quotable formulations of cultural theory, statements that both dignify literary criticism and encourage critics to become more than just literary. In his frequently cited essay "Blurred Genres: The Refiguration of Social Thought," Geertz asserts that the social sciences must turn to the humanities for an improved notion of culture and a new method: "the casting of social theory in terms more familiar to gamesters and aestheticians than to plumbers and engineers is well under way. The recourse to the humanities for explanatory analogies in the social sciences is at once evidence of the destabilization of genres and of the rise of 'the interpretive turn'" (168). Elsewhere, Geertz often asserts that anthropologists should use interpretative strategies characteristic of literary criticism: "Analysis, then, is sorting out the structures of signification—what Ryle called established codes, a somewhat misleading expression, for it makes the enterprise sound too much like that of the cipher clerk when it is much like that of the literary critic—and determining their social ground and import" (*Interpretation of Cultures*, 9); "Meaning, that elusive and ill-defined pseudoentity we were once more than content to leave to philosophers and literary critics to fumble with, has now come back into the heart of our discipline" (29).

Literary criticism, then, has something to teach the social sciences. Literary critics are, in fact, as engaged in culture as anthropologists are. Geertz says in a footnote that his anthropology sets out to "deprovincialize" the concept of art and denies any aesthetic that places art "beyond the reach of sociological analysis" (*Interpretation of Cultures*, 451), but he still preserves aesthetic categories, leaving literary critics (if anthropologically "deprovincialized") a certified field of action. In Geertz's interpretive anthropology, literary scholars can implement their humanities training and carry out semi-social science inquiries. In Geertz's epigrammatic shifts from social mechanics to social semantics, from empirical description to analogical speculation, humanities scholars find a resolution to their expertise in poetics and their desire to speak of culture. The fact that his positions are highly controversial in the field of anthropology and that no anthropologist would take his statements so piously as does Greenblatt ("Geertz is too thoughtful and canny a writer . . . "; "Geertz's words have a well-crafted rhetorical effect"; "it is no particular surprise to learn from Geertz that . . . "—"Eating of the Soul," 97, 97, 99) is no matter. Indeed, to enter into anthropological debates about Geertz's work would only lessen his authority. Cultural poetics takes from Geertz a set of motives and premises, not arguments and demonstrations. With the former securely in hand, cultural poetics can proceed confidently to textual readings that now have social and cultural significance.

cultural studies   What is cultural studies? Though it may be one of the hottest areas of inquiry today, many teachers and scholars are not quite sure what cultural studies really is. Despite the fact that whole books are devoted to the subject (like John Storey's volume *What Is Cultural Studies? A Reader* and Patrick Brantlinger's survey *Crusoe's Footprints: Cultural Studies in Britain and America*), the enterprise remains indeterminate to professors and students not directly involved in it. One would expect that a reading of cultural studies anthologies or journals would impart to curious readers what cultural studies does, what methods it follows, what objects it interprets. But a scan of cultural studies' titles, subject matters, and approaches reveals so much diversity of interests and methods that a categorical description of cultural studies cannot be derived from them.

Even in general outlines of cultural studies, one often finds an exasperating variety of scholarly traits. For example, in the editorial statement of *Cultural Studies* (1996), a leading American journal in the field, one might expect to find a concise institutional summation of what materials and methods are appropriate to cultural studies work. But instead, the statement contains a meandering list of concerns and strategies that do not coalesce into a discrete inquiry.

[T]he journal seeks work that explores the relation between everyday life, cultural practices, and material, economic, political, geographical and historical contexts; that understands cultural studies as an analytic of social change; that addresses a widening range of topic areas, including post- and neo-colonial relations, the politics of popular culture, issues in nationality, transnationality and globalization, the performance of gendered, sexual, and queer identities, and the organization of power around differences in race, class, ethnicity, etc.; that reflects on the status of cultural studies; and that pursues the theoretical implications and underpinnings of practical inquiry and critique. (no page number)

If this is an accurate demarcation of cultural studies, one wonders not what cultural studies is but what it is not. Because cultural studies covers everyday life, cultural practices, economics, politics, geography, history, race, class, ethnicity, theory and practice, gender, sexuality, and power, the things it includes number more than the things it excludes. The only types of humanities and social science inquiry not applicable to cultural studies are aesthetics, logic, and metaphysics. In terms of subject matter, everything else in the humanities and social sciences has the potential to fit this editorial solicitation. Moving from the uselessly general ("everyday life, cultural practices") to the fashionably particular ("the performance of . . . queer identities"), the statement jumps randomly from one topic to the next, as it suggests cultural studies itself does ("that addresses a widening range of topic areas"). Moreover, in terms of method, cultural studies apparently has no interpretative practices that are specific to it. The above outline gives no indication as to how cultural studies researchers proceed, what conditions it requires, what analytic tools it uses. (The characterization of cultural studies as "an analytic of social change" provides little help here.) Whether cultural studies is theoretical or practical, empirical or speculative, textual or material—such determinations are missing. The only methodological guideline *Cultural Studies* offers is a resolute but murky disdain for formalism and idealism.

No wonder students and scholars remain confused as to the identity of cultural studies. Indeed, the difficulty of defining cultural studies begins with its title, or rather, in the obscurity of its title's reference. What does the term signify? Some might say it denotes the Birmingham school style of analysis of subcultures in capitalist societies (Raymond Williams, E. P. Thompson, Stuart Hall). Others might point to a Frankfurt School critique of Enlightenment ideals in cultural contexts or to a Baudrillardean diagnosis of the "class logic" implicit in consumer society. In such conceptions, the practice would seem to possess a method, a subject matter, and a goal sufficiently specific to constitute a distinct area of inquiry with a disciplinary focus. In these versions, inquirers outside the field would recognize it in action and understand its provenance. But in those cases, a more precise field label than "cultural studies" would seem necessary, at least to help scholars and students identify the purview of the inquiry. Why not call it "the sociology of consumption" or "capitalism and subculture studies"? If these terms are declared to be too narrow, if the term "cultural studies" signifies broadly "criticism of culture," then one wonders, culture as opposed to what? Criticism of non-culture? If cultural studies criticism is the social and political analysis of events, artifacts, and commodities as cultural texts doing cultural work, does that mean it is opposed to analysis of texts doing natural work? What disciplinary practice in the humanities and social sciences does not already entail criticism of culture, or rather, of some institutionally demarcated portion of culture?

If scholars and critics are impatient with those demarcations, then they may draw new ones and argue for their institutionalization. But how does one establish an institution of cultural studies without quickly setting up sub-institutions organized around categories of language, history, nationality, and aesthetics? Traditionally, disciplines naturally fell into acknowledged subdivisions, for example, as literary criticism broke up into formalist literary criticism, philological criticism, narratological analysis, and other methodologically distinguished pursuits, all of which remained comfortably within the category "literary criticism." But cultural studies eschews such institutional disjunctions and will not let any straitening adjective precede the "cultural studies" heading. There is no distinct formalist cultural studies or historicist cultural studies, but only cultural studies. (Feminist cultural studies may be one exception.) Cultural studies is a field that will not be parceled out to the available disciplines. It spans culture at large, not this or that institutionally separated element of culture. To guarantee this transcendence of disciplinary institutions, cultural studies must select a name for itself that has no specificity, that has too great an extension to mark off any expedient boundaries for itself. "Cultural studies" serves well because, apart from distinguishing between "physical science" and "cultural analysis," the term provides no indication of where any other boundaries lie.

This is exactly the point. To blur disciplinary boundaries and frustrate the intellectual investments that go along with them is a fundamental motive for cultural studies practice, one that justifies the vagueness of the titular term. This explains why the related label "cultural criticism," so much in vogue in 1988, has declined. The term "criticism" has a narrower extension than does "studies," ruling out some empirical forms of inquiry (like field work) that "studies" admits. "Studies" preserves a methodological openness that "criticism" closes. Since such closures have suspect political intentions behind them, cultural studies maintains its institutional purity by disdaining disciplinary identity and methodological uniformity. (See Stanley Fish's *Professional Correctness* for an astute analysis of this claim and its pragmatic untenability.) Even when a piece of cultural criticism accords with a well-known tradition like that of Birmingham, it resists easy categorization of method and discipline. The editors of a cultural studies anthology openly proclaim that "It is problematic for cultural studies simply to adopt, uncritically, any of the formalized disciplinary practices of the academy, for those practices, as much as the distinctions they inscribe, carry with them a heritage of disciplinary investments and exclusions and a history of social effects that cultural studies would often be inclined to repudiate" (Grossberg, Nelson, and Treichler, 1–2; this refusal of methodological specificity is echoed often in cultural studies announcements). So no methodology can either be "privileged" or "eliminated. . . . Textual analysis, semiotics, deconstruction, ethnography, interviews, phonemic analysis, psychoanalysis, rhizomatics, content analysis, survey research—all can provide important insights and knowledge" (2). One suspects the list of types of inquiry could go on much longer. This motley interdisciplinarity endows inquiry with freedom and generosity, for the more cultural studies inquirers can mobilize a host of methods and foci into an interpretation, the more they overcome the exclusions of any single approach. The plurality of practices shields inquirers from disciplinary cooptation, drawing researchers away from the demands of their research institutions and bringing them closer to the culture they study. A single approach will miss too much, will overlook important aspects of culture not perceptible to that particular angle of vision. A multitude of approaches will pick up an insight here and a piece of knowledge there and more of culture will enter into the inquiry. A diversity of methods will match the diversity of culture, thereby sheltering the true nature of culture from the reductive appropriations of formal disciplines.

But how do cultural critics bring all these methods together into a coherent inquiry? Are there any established rules of incorporating "important insights and knowledge" coming out of different methods into a coherent scholarly project of cultural studies? How might a scholar use both phonemic analysis and deconstruction in a single inquiry when deconstructionist arguments call into question the basic premises of phonetics? What scholar has the competence to handle materials from so many disciplines in a rigorous and knowing manner? Does cultural criticism as a "studies" practice offer any transdisciplinary evaluative standards to apply to individual pieces of cultural criticism? If not, if there is no clear methodological procedures or evaluative principles in cultural studies, it is hard to see how one might popularize it, teach it, make it into a recognized scholarly activity. In practical terms, one does not know how to communicate it to others or show students how to do it when it assumes so many different methodological forms. How does one create an academic department out of an outspokenly anti-disciplinary practice? What criteria can faculty members jointly invoke when they are trying to make curricular and personnel decisions?

Once again, this is precisely the point. One reason for the generality of the term is to render such institutional questions unanswerable. Cultural studies practice mingles methods from a variety of fields, jumps from one cultural subject matter to another, simultaneously proclaims superiority to other institutionalized inquiries (on a correspondence to culture basis) and renounces its own institutionalization—gestures that strategically forestall disciplinary standards being applied to it. By studying culture in heterogenous ways, by clumping texts, events, persons, objects, and ideologies into a cultural whole (which, cultural critics say, is reality) and bringing a melange of logical argument, speculative propositions, empirical data, and political outlooks to bear upon it, cultural critics invent a new kind of investigation immune to methodological attack. A logician's discovery of a fallacy, a literary critic's discovery of a misreading, a historian's discovery of a false causality—such disciplinary-based criticisms will not apply to an inquiry rearranging disciplinary bits and pieces into an improved representation. Prizing truth to culture over formal validity, cultural studies celebrates its periodic disregard for uniform methods as a necessity of accurate renditions of culture. The term "cultural studies" well suits that anti-methodological need. Any further specification of it might satisfy a requirement of success in the academy, but would hinder cultural studies' fidelity to the public sphere. The multiple references of the term, then, mark a resistance to academic identity and a heightened engagement with extra-academic politics and society. If cultural studies chose a term that named a specific scholarly practice, the term would distinguish that practice's methods, subject matter, and goals from those of other practices. The resulting disciplinary identity would include a set of protocols and formalities that places limits on the work critics do. Instead of being free-ranging intellectuals truthfully representing culture, critics would become specialists formally completing disciplinary tasks. The term "cultural studies" ensures against that impoverishment. Therefore, the question "what is cultural studies?" if intended as a search for a unified field with a discrete method, is inapt. Further clarification must not happen. The term "cultural studies" thrives on the multifariousness of its reference.

decisive assertions   "Decisive assertions" covers not a term but an argumentative habit. It sometimes seems as if the mark of critical aptitude is to couch one's general statements, descriptions, or interpretations, debatable though they may be, in an air of indisputability. To be assertive in one's premises and conclusions, utterly positive of one's positionings—that is the sign of critical acuity. The fact that the premises remain largely unsubstantiated and the conclusions unproven easily goes unnoticed when scholarship is cloaked in a rhetoric of canniness and certainty. When critics become so sure of their material, especially when the material is composed not of concrete historical facts, but of cultural texts, bewildering theories, and knotty political contexts, then one hesitates to question their statements. The contentions, however speculative, seem to be offered up to readers not for analysis, discussion, or assessment, but only for acquiescence.

One feature of critical imperiousness is its tendency toward sweeping historical generalizations, magisterial political summations, or simplistic identifications of *x* with *y*. Countless arguments that begin or end with references to, say, "the politics of individualism," "the Romantic paradigm," or "the complicitousness of postmodernism" regularly throw diverse phenomena and concepts onto a categorical heap, usually without elucidating the discrete referents falling into the category. Sometimes the generalization takes the form of an ideological aside on some school or thought, as when one critic mentions "the modernist and New Critical insistence on the separation of politics and art," as if such generalizations were patent truths (Erkkila, 54). At other times the assertion appears as a monolithic narrative explanation for historical change, as when Gerald Graff attributes the rise of "indeterminacy" as a literary value to the following cause:

> The growth of empirical science and the expansion of industrial, commercial, and technological forms of society after the mid-eighteenth century thus encouraged a way of thinking about the indeterminacy of literature that was different from earlier ways. As modern science and commerce identified themselves with the procedures of clear, distinct thought and practical efficiency, it seemed natural for poets and literary critics to claim a special affinity with the more shadowy, undefined, and elusive regions of consciousness that science and commerce tended to ignore or undervalue. The poetic or literary function thus came more and more to be defined as an alternative to the unambiguous clarity promoted by scientists, businessmen, and engineers. (164)

Still other pronouncements take the form of an incontestable definition, as when Paul de Man offers his characterization of "ideology": "What we call ideology is precisely the confusion of linguistic with natural reality, of reference with phenomenalism" (11). Finally, one often sees huge inferences pulled from the slightest of materials, as when Judith Butler notes the female impersonator Divine's performance in a John Waters film and claims, "His/her performance destabilizes the very distinctions between the natural and the artificial, depth and surface, inner and outer through which discourse about genders almost always operates"

(*Gender Trouble*, x). Or when Kaja Silverman declares that "my present concern in this chapter will be to trace the consequences for masculinity of a particular historical upheaval—that of World War II and the recovery period" (52), and then offers not a speck of historical research, but instead proceeds to analyze *Beyond the Pleasure Principle* and three postwar films, as if those four pieces encapsulated the period. Whether categorical, anecdotal, or axiomatic, these kinds of wholesale judgments do not often derive from or enhance a deliberate analysis of contexts, texts, or terms. Indeed, in their haste to posit a comprehensive understanding of difficult concepts like "ideology" and "indeterminacy" and multifarious events like "modernism," "gender," and "postwar masculinity," these generalizing critics simply take for granted the numerous historical particulars and rival opinions that might, at the very least, complicate their generalizations.

Butler's assertion that Divine's impersonation destabilizes natural-artificial, depth-surface, inner-outer distinctions is a remarkable piece of bombast. Without any evidence or premises, she lays the burden of undoing the major distinctions of Western thought upon Divine's film role. In Waters's film, the founding concepts of philosophy collapse, nature and artifice become performative constructs, depth and surface and inner and outer become fluid polarities, all because a man puts on a dress. One wonders if, as he applied his make-up, Divine knew he was presiding over the demise of Western metaphysics.

In the Erkkila case, does every modernist writer and New Critic separate politics and art? As for the "insistence" noted: does she argue against it? Do modernists and New Critics assert the separation as an ontological proposition or a historical truth, or do they offer the separation on pedagogical, methodological, personal, or pragmatic grounds? How does the claim bear upon texts like Pound's *Guide to Kulchur*, Eliot's *After Strange Gods*, or the volume *I'll Take My Stand*? Without any contexts for understanding the insistence, we have no way of knowing the basis and extent of the modernists' and New Critics' claim. If we accept the observation that modernists and New Critics insisted that politics and art were separate, we still have no idea why they did so and what evidence or premises they invoked to support the distinction. Erkkila sees no need to provide any further information.

Graff's historical mini-narrative suffers from a similar absence of context and specificity. We might excuse the simplifications because they appear in a book of essays on critical terminology, the kind of reference work that gives scholars license to generalize. But the interpretation Graff pushes is a matter of historical truth, not of definition of terms, so his statements call for some historical interrogation. Graff bases his judgment on the inference that, as science and commerce embraced clear and efficient objectivity, "it seemed natural" for poets to embrace shadowy subjectivity. That is the genesis of indeterminacy. But the insight that y "seems naturally" to follow x hardly qualifies as a demonstration of historical causality. With so many variables in play, historical causality is a tricky enough thing to prove even when one has mountains of facts and texts to make inductions from. To substantiate the assertion that indeterminacy stems from Romantic subjectivity, which in turn stems from technological objectivity, one would have to call upon explicit phenomena in support of the sequence. For example, in formulations of Romantic "shadowiness," we should find express and consistent statements of opposition to technology. In postulations of indeterminacy, we should find that indeterminacy is repeatedly located in a subjective realm. Even in a glossary of critical terms, one can offer some documentation. One can, at the very least, indicate the necessity of such documentation and how and where one can find the sources. Or one can acknowledge the partiality of the explanation.

In any case, the indiscriminate inferences and hidden premises entailed by assertions of this sort remain implicit, tacitly affirmed but unexamined. Nevertheless, the argument proceeds smoothly, for this kind of scholarship aims at a macrocriticism, a profile of the Big Picture. The broad assertions critics produce are supposed to stand as momentous interpretations, decisive conceptualizations that comprehend all historical particulars and texts within a new and satisfying way of seeing. Of course, defining literary classifications and cultural contexts has always played a role in literary scholarship. But what distinguishes many recent critics' large categorizations is a lack of historical backing or logical analysis accompanying them. Seldom are the general statements accompanied by copious historical evidence or scrupulous deductive reasoning. The macrocritic's entire project seems to be the Big Picture, a task requiring him not to throw himself into the particulars comprising it but to abstract himself from them, to frame the picture as a whole.

In the critic's hands, modernism, ideology, the eighteenth century, structuralism, or any other scholarly subject matter is not something to study, analyze, or explore. Rather, it is something to situate, to position. The conceptual complexities and historical genesis of, for example, modernism are contained, simplified, or outright ignored by the critic's subsuming interpretative acts. Whether that comprehension is due to the critic's superior knowledge, his capacious awareness, her Derridean grasp of the history of Western metaphysics, his Foucauldean sensitivity to power/knowledge relations, her feminist suspicion of patriarchal strategies, his postcolonial recognition of imperialist discourse, the result is all too often the same. Unsupported propositions stand as legitimate premises.

Let us test the strength of *that* generalization by analyzing the last of the examples cited above. Erkkila's comment is too cursory to merit analytical discussion. Graff's statement, again, appears in an essay on critical terminology and, although the rest of his piece contains no empirical facts to support his historical summary, the genre may justify some measure of generalization. Butler's comment is too polemically based and Silverman's too historiographically embarrassing to warrant extensive comment. So, take the example from de Man: "What we call ideology is precisely the confusion of linguistic with natural reality, of reference with phenomenalism." Christopher Norris has said that this and the following sentence "would stand a good deal of conceptual unpacking" (10; Norris does not supply the unpacking). The sentence has a nice resounding parallel syntax, a clear and authoritative contrast of often confused terms (though whether the sentence is a stipulation or a description is unclear). Indeed, it makes the confusion "precise," isolates it and gives it a name: "ideology." Out of the heretofore vague use of the term—"What we call"—comes a stark definition of "ideology" in sharp conceptual oppositions and imposing philosophical terms, a definition made even more powerful by the fact that it defines "ideology" itself and thereby seems immune to ideological criticism. Like many of de Man's pronouncements, it fixes an overdetermined term's meaning with rigor and authority, judiciousness and power. Debates over the nature of this or that ideology, over what its effects are, over what causal relations exist between this ideology and that institution, and so on, may continue, but what ideology is at bottom de Man has pinpointed with exactitude and wisdom.

However, notwithstanding the rhetorical force of de Man's definition, does it stand up to analysis? Do the pieces hang together logically as well as they do syntactically?

First, the "is." Does de Man mean ideology *is* the "confusion," is the exact same thing as "the confusion of linguistic with natural reality"? Are the terms entirely synonymous? De Man's phrasing indicates they are. But in what way can ideology *be* a confusion of two things? If de Man means that ideology always rests upon or stems from a confusion of linguistic reality with natural reality, then his connection of one with the other makes some sense (which is not to say that it is truthful or useful). But if that is the case, why does de Man identify ideology precisely as a confusion of realities, and not as some kind of system of ideas in some causal, logical, or historical relation to that confusion? Until de Man clarifies whether he is equating ideology itself with the confusion (and showing how that works) or simply marking ideology's reliance upon the confusion, the point of his statement remains obscure.

Next: "linguistic reality" and "natural reality." What does "linguistic reality" denote? Is it the reality of language? Probably not. The epithet suggests some predication of "reality" by "language," but not in the sense of posing something "real" about language as opposed to something "unreal" about it. Rather, the term likely refers to the reality language refers to, the reality rendered intelligible by language. This "linguistic reality," then, contrasts with a "non-linguistic reality," a reality unstructured by any language system— namely, "natural reality." Presumably, "natural reality" denotes a reality not reducible to linguistic categories. "Natural reality" is reality itself, reality unmediated by any system of signs, unconstituted by anything but itself. Whereas "linguistic reality" implies a relation of two disparate things, language and reality, "natural reality" implies a coincidence of two identical things, nature and reality. Hence, within the generality of de Man's description, the concept "natural reality" is something of a redundancy. And "linguistic reality" is something of a contradiction, in that it makes reality itself conditional upon a language, an assertion inconsistent with reality's basic denotation of "what there is."

I used the vague word "something" in the previous two sentences and supplied a reference for "reality" because of a vagueness in de Man's own handling of "reality." For the indiscriminateness of his contrast solicits from readers a clarification of his terms, and the last part of his definition does little to narrow down his meaning: "of reference with phenomenalism." It is unclear how "reference," a word denoting an act of referring or a thing referred to, can be confused with "phenomenalism," a philosophical belief stating that what we know depends on acts of consciousness, that the ultimate nature of reality is unknowable, that all knowledge originates in perception, and so on. The two terms are so far apart as to be un-confusable, even un-opposable, and the only place I have ever seen the terms in "confusion" is here. Now, it is true that the syntax aligns "reference" with "linguistic reality" and "phenomenalism" with "natural reality." Also, the preceding paragraph contains the phrase "natural or phenomenal cognition," another obscure predication but one that does link "natural" with "phenomenal." Perhaps de Man intends to contrast phenomenalism and its emphasis on a mental ordering of reality with something like "referentialism" and its emphasis on a linguistic ordering of reality. But the distinction is not as sharp as de Man would have it, since phenomenalism posits a "natural reality" only insofar as it is mediated and organized by the senses, by habits of seeing, by categories of the understanding, and so on. One might say that those structures of consciousness are more natural in an epistemological sense than those of language, but if in fact de Man wishes to push that formulation, he does not elaborate upon it any further.

Given these terminological problems, the best unambiguous paraphrase one can make of de Man's statement is: ideology entails a belief in natural reality, specifically, a naive trust that one can see through systems of reference and grasp the independent reality beyond them. Exactly how the naïveté yields or *is* ideology is left unsaid. The idea may be a tantalizing one, but in de Man's essay it remains unexpounded, just as the terms he uses to express the point themselves are just provocative enough to inspire fascination but slippery enough to prevent conclusive understanding.

Obviously, this piece by piece inquest into a sentence by de Man does not invalidate the entire argument of his essay, nor does it show that de Man's sentence is wrong. Instead, the analysis reveals the incomplete, inarticulate status of the sentence and, hence, of any argument based upon it. De Man's statement begs too many questions and uses too many undefined terms for it to sustain an argument about ideology, language, and reality. The meanings of "is," "reality," and "reference" are here too inchoate or ambiguous for one to draw inferences from their usage with any certainty. If de Man elucidated his terms and clarified the dual contrast he poses, then one could determine the accuracy or truth or consistency of his statement. But as it stands, not even its import can be determined clearly.

Herein lies the rhetorical advantage of such blanket general propositions, be they stipulative or descriptive: they are so characteristically all-inclusive, so expressly imprecise that one cannot specify their exact meaning or reference, much less decide their truth or falsity or utility. Too abstract to be verified empirically, too vague to be explicated logically, assertions like "What we call ideology . . . " claim truth by virtue of their assertiveness. If the terms were more clearly defined and their extension less comprehensive, one would be able to verify them—or falsify them. But in their current hazy state, one can assert their truth only by faith and their falsity only by a counterassertiveness. This is the strategic value of summary assertions. They grant the critic a seeming mastery over his material and they shield him or her from refutation. They contain enough generality to evince the critic's erudition, but not enough specific content to be proven wrong. Their largesse is approbative, their obscurity is protective.

deconstruction   The term "deconstruction" initially signified a specific type of conceptual analysis developed by Jacques Derrida. In his early works, Derrida applied deconstruction to the master concepts of Western metaphysics (presence, identity, voice, consciousness) in order to explore their complex structure and to map their dialectical workings and tacit elements. Specifically, deconstructive analysis aimed to reveal within those putatively fundamental concepts their implicit conceptual other (alterity, difference, writing, the unconscious), the repressed and opposed concepts that, though contrary to the master concepts, are nevertheless necessary to the master concepts' definition and use. What distinguished deconstructive analysis from other forms of conceptual analysis was the analytic tool Derrida derived from his precursors: *différance*. A modification of Martin Heidegger's ontic-ontological difference (as "deconstruction" is a modification of Heidegger's *destruktion*) and of Ferdinand de Saussure's semiotic difference, *différance* was Derrida's definitive intervention into the history of metaphysics and the characteristic argumentative trait of deconstruction. In the phenomenological and structuralist traditions Derrida worked within (analytic philosophy remains largely untouched by Derridean thinking), scholars now had to account for the decisive revision *différance* created in philosophical analysis. Those who found *différance* a worthwhile conceptual invention and implemented it in their own scholarship and teaching could call themselves deconstructive critics. But if an analysis did not invoke *différance* or any of its variants (like the "supplement"), then it could not qualify as a deconstruction.

This "differantial" feature of deconstruction has disappeared from contemporary usage. The rather arcane philosophical context of the term "deconstruction" no longer shapes critics' understanding of what "deconstruction" means or is. While early votaries of deconstruction (J. Hillis Miller, Joseph N. Riddel, and others) were already steeped in Friedrich Nietzsche, Edmund Husserl, Heidegger, and other Continental figures by the time Derrida arrived, today's purveyors of deconstruction often manifest little awareness of the Continental background. When teaching deconstruction, doing a deconstructive reading, or attributing deconstructiveness to other arguments and texts, critics rarely call upon the philosophical or linguistic baggage the term carries. Hardly ever does one find Husserl's *Logical Investigations*, Alexandre Kojève's *Introduction to the Reading of Hegel*, or Heidegger's *Early Greek Thinking* on theory course syllabi. When citing Derrida on metaphysical concepts like the subject, critics generally overlook the variations of subjectivity in René Descartes, Immanuel Kant, Nietzsche, and Jacques Lacan, within all of which Derrida has framed his own notion of subjectivity. This neglect of philosophical context would not cause so many promiscuous usages of "deconstruction" were it not for the fact that the context is precisely what maintains the singularity of deconstructive analysis. For the distinctive meaning of "deconstruction" lies in what it derives from, which is why Derrida's important essay "Différance" develops, in part, through extensions of "differential" concepts in Nietzsche, Saussure, Heidegger, and Freud. What distinguish deconstructive analysis from other forms of analysis are the concepts of difference that deconstruction has adopted and radicalized. Forget those precedents and one blurs deconstruction together with other types of textual analysis.

This is what has happened to the term "deconstruction." Instead of an ontological or linguistic context shaping the term's significance, a new context and import now prevails: the political. "Deconstruction" now means, simply, "analysis with a political force." A deconstruction is now an analysis that exposes some politically repressed concept, group, figure, or event and thereby exposes a political motivation behind the repression. When Henry A. Giroux says in "Consuming Social Change: The 'United Colors of Benetton'" that he "will attempt to deconstruct three of [Benetton's] more politically charged photojournalistic advertisements" (8— the ads are pictures of black-white intimacy), all he means is that he will reveal that it "is precisely the absent referents of resistance, rupture, and critique that allow the reader to be perfectly comfortable with such a configuration of race and class while at the same time accepting the image as nothing more than a 'playful' ad" (25). He makes implicit political meanings and ambiguities explicit, brings "absent referents" to presence. That is all. When David Damrosch says of a book on New World conquest that it "use[s] a close study of the conquistadores' language to deconstruct the ambitions of empire itself" (516) and never mentions another word on deconstruction, all he means is that the book exposes the conquistadores' ideological blindnesses and rationalizations.

In these typical examples, Derrida's conceptual analysis has turned into a political diagnosis. An analysis that reveals political machinations and ideological suppositions subtly at work within a discourse becomes a "deconstruction." Feminists expose and attack patriarchy, postmodernists parody Romantic and Modernist aesthetics, Marxists analyze commodity fetishism, postcolonialists demythologize imperialism, theorists demystify natural attitudes and essentialist predications. Although these strategies all antedate deconstruction, "deconstruct" is often the verb used to describe them. Feminist, postmodernist, and other analyses dismantle putatively objective hierarchies, show the constructedness of all universalist claims, demonstrate the structural necessity of things marginalized, and these revelations undo various political repressions. So, they are deconstructions.

But where does *différance* appear in these politico-theoretical analyses? What ontology of alterity shapes the critique? How do presence, Being, transcendence, Spirit, and the Book, notions Derrida has consistently addressed, figure in political unveilings of marginality and otherness? Political diagnoses of texts deal with inscribed political realities, not abstract metaphysical concepts. Though the inscription of politics may follow conditions in part organized by metaphysical concepts and though the reification of those concepts serves political purposes, the political analysis of this or that text aims not to rehearse the dialectical mechanisms of *différance*, but to clarify the practical political differences the text encodes, exemplifies, subverts, critiques, and otherwise "deconstructs." To one familiar with the early texts of Derrida, deconstruction would seem to be too abstract to serve such political ends. As Eve Sedgwick puts it, "Deconstruction, founded as a very science of *differ(e/a)nce*, has both so fetishized the idea of difference and so vaporized its possible embodiments that its most thoroughgoing practitioners are the last people to whom one would now look for help in thinking about particular differenc*es*" (*Epistemology of the Closet*, 23). This is not to say that deconstruction has no political possibilities in the desired sense. Deconstruction does bring to the surface many buried assumptions and concepts, and it is possible to apply deconstructive strategies to social, political, and institutional situations. (Sam Weber's *Institution and Interpretation* is one such example.) But, strictly speaking, the real world application remains deconstructive precisely by implementing the conceptual tool kit unique to deconstruction. Deconstruction reveals sedimented attitudes and principles, but so does any kind of dialectical commentary. The uncovering of otherness, of the other that constitutes the thing, the self, the identity as such, dates back to Hegel and is basic to any dialectical discourse. Divorced from that Hegelian tradition and undifferentiated from other strategies in that tradition, the attribution of "deconstruction" to all otherly directed analyses stems not from a respect for deconstruction's dialectical heritage, but rather from the political meaning now attached to the term. If deconstruction now signifies a distinctive form of analysis, the distinctiveness comes not from a philosophical tradition, but from a political strategy.

So why call them "deconstructions"? Political investigations of texts—commentaries bringing out the politically repressed other—are already politically meritorious and intellectually illuminating, so why add to them a name denoting a complex conceptual analysis and recalling an unrelated philosophical tradition?

Three reasons.

First, the attribution of "deconstructive" to political interpretation draws an analytical tool of criticism out of the metaphysical clouds. In translating deconstruction's old metaphysical alterities (like presence-absence) into ideological alterities (like colonizer-native), critics convert deconstruction from a rarefied textual explication to an engaged political exposé. (Gayatri Spivak's *The Post-Colonial Critic* contains numerous examples of how Derridean propositions about writing, otherness, and positionality can be recast into explicit political terms and still retain some speculative flavor.) Once cured of its vaporish metaphysical interests, deconstruction no longer seems like a sterile formalism, a refurbished New Criticism, a mandarin theory of reading stuck in intertextual playfulness. When applied to concrete political structures and their embedded assumptions and exclusions, deconstruction's inventive interpretative maneuvers have real world relevance and consequence. Indeed, if politics is not just the actual mobilization of groups but also the construction of group identities, the circulation of group representations, the writing of group values and meanings upon bodies, institutions, technologies, and other material realities, then a seemingly esoteric textual strategy like deconstruction would be eminently useful to political analysis. The politicization of deconstruction would mirror the textualization of politics. If deconstruction can provide a significant political critique, then the deconstructive critic can have his or her theory and practice at the same time.

This retailoring of the deconstructive theorist into a politically active, socially observant critic leads to the second advantage of the term "deconstruction." By adding an intricate textual keyword like "deconstruction" to political interpretation, critics elevate their intellectual status. If the political critique is a deconstruction, the critic becomes more than just a partisan or a pundit. Deconstruction is too cerebral to serve crass political designs, too scholastic to sink into polemics, too complex to function as political attack or endorsement. The term grants critics a more than mere political discernment and professionalism—although, of course, "deconstruction" does not imply a complete divestment of political concerns. It only lifts critics out of an unsophisticated political investment.

The word dignifies political analysis, gives a philosophical cachet to political judgment. It helps critics know the ways of political machinations, the political effects that can operate at textual levels (through discourse) and that only a textual strategy as canny as deconstruction can identify. As a deconstruction, political analysis sounds technical and learned, even though its genuine technicality (phenomenological and structuralist) has subsided. What remains is a political acumen, an interpreter's capacity to identify various political commitments the writer has unwittingly left traces of in the text.

Herein lies the third advantage of "deconstruction" politically considered: its capacity to expose ideological lies, to dismantle cultural cover-ups. Derrida's readings of Rousseau, Husserl, et al. in *Of Grammatology* and *Speech and Phenomena* disclosed implicit exclusions operating in their texts and subtly structuring their positions. His analysis of center-margin dynamics in "Structure, Sign, and Play in the Discourse of the Human Sciences" and *Disseminations* revealed contradictions and paradoxes at the root of philosophical systems, those logical problems usually revolving around the attempt to neutralize difference. In devising hermeneutical methods that highlighted a text's tactical exclusions and disguised differentiations, Derrida bequeathed to critics the means of exploring a political situation's repressed others. If deconstruction could divulge the exclusion of semiotic difference from Husserl's theory of meaning, then it could also reveal the exclusion of racial difference, sexual difference, and cultural difference from this or that political context. No matter how cleverly a political logistics dispensed with an other, no matter how smoothly the ideological apparatus coped with the other's decentering effects, a politically improved deconstruction could recount the stigmatization and bring the other back to parity with the privileged one. Hence, even though many political critics find Paul de Man's work to be immorally unresponsive to political circumstances, even de Man himself could claim that "the linguistics of literariness [i.e., deconstructive literary theory] is a powerful and indispensable tool in the unmasking of ideological aberrations" (*Resistance to Theory*, 11). It only takes a simple substitution of a political other for deconstruction's metaphysical other for criticism to salvage deconstructive theory from apolitical pretensions.

These three benefits of political "deconstruction"—the escape from metaphysics, the elevation of political discussion, the incisiveness of interpretation—make the term attractive to critics taught to analyze texts, yet striving for extratextual involvements with politics. While it is true that the politicization of deconstruction entails a loss of conceptual specificity, an adherence to deconstruction's philosophical background will only mire critics in abstruse metaphysical debates. A non-political deconstructive analysis may be logically correct, but institutionally unwanted and morally dubious in the current climate of inquiry. The rhetorical and personal gains of a political usage of "deconstruction" are too certain to pass up.

discipline A classic study published in 1972 by the Organization for Economic Co-operation and Development defines "discipline" as a "specific body of teachable knowledge with its own background of education, training procedures, methods and content areas" (*Interdisciplinarity: Problems of Teaching and Research in Universities*, 25). Another well-known statement, by Joseph J. Kockelmans, assigns to a discipline three elements: one, "the educational process that implies both teaching and learning"; two, "the subject matter of that process"; and three, "the training of scholars to proper and orderly action within the realm of a science" ("Science and Discipline," 16–17). Finally, a 1990 book by Julie Thompson Klein on interdisciplinarity says, "The term *discipline* signifies tools, methods, procedures, exempla, concepts, and theories that account coherently for a set of objects or subjects" (*Interdisciplinarity*, 104). Each of these definitions of "discipline" emphasizes method as a distinguishing feature of any discipline. A discipline exists as a discrete enterprise of study both because it interprets a particular content—"content areas," "subject matter," "a set of objects or subjects"—and because it has a unique approach to that content: "training procedures, methods," "proper and orderly action within the realm of a science," "tools . . . concepts, and theories." Disciplines have methodological protocols that inquirers must accord with if they expect their work to qualify as disciplinary. The objects selected for study only partly demarcate the disciplinary boundary. Added to them is an assembly of concepts, a procedure for gathering materials, a manner of interpreting them, and other research instruments and methods that "account" for the object, and the measure of their propriety is not accuracy to the object, but coherence with one another. Indeed, in the second definition, the subject matter is not even separable from the "educational process," but is rather "the subject matter *of that process.*"

In an essay from 1970 on "Theory in the Humanities and Sociology," Talcott Parsons adds to the coherence standard of disciplinarity the criterion of empirical validity. Validity is a quality derived from the structure of knowledge, not from the truth of a piece of knowledge or from the reality of the object. Hence, he argues, the discrimination of disciplines must come from the methods proper to each particular field:

[A]s modes of action oriented to valid knowledge, the disciplines (German *Wissenschaften*) share the primacy of the values of cognitive rationality, but the modes of implementation of these values vary as a function of the type of object studied, the type of interest manifested, the variety of data available, and the method appropriate for such study. (495)

Since "cognitive rationality" is common to all disciplines, methods bear an even greater burden of differentiating one discipline from another. All disciplines operate by "modes of action" producing "valid knowledge," while each discipline achieves its own knowledge through distinct and fixed "modes of implementation." The requirement of cognitive rationality means that disciplinary knowledge must be cognizable in systematic, repeatable ways. (This is why something like the writing of poetry, which may have its own goals and methods, still can never be a discipline in this sense, since cognitive rationality is not necessarily part of its creative domain. Only when the experience of poetry is broached on a cognitive rational basis, namely, through criticism, can poetry become a disciplinary object.) On these rational grounds, where inquiry follows orderly methods to produce recognizable knowledge, objects, data, judgments, and interests come to have disciplinary import. So, in disciplinary acts interest is not just interest per se, but sociological interest or literary critical interest or psychological interest. "Object" in a sociological context means something different from "object" in a literary critical context. The contents of disciplinary inquiry are submitted to a customary practice, to disciplinary conventions that, in fact, distinguish one discipline from another more than the studied objects do. These distinctions, Parsons says, must be understood as "general methodological issues" (499). They do not rest upon any particular perception, result, or motive, but upon a fundamental methodological divergence that yields incongruous disciplinary wholes.

Such method-oriented understandings of discipline explain the current unpopularity of the term "disciplinary." Because disciplines thrive on the consistent exercise of hermeneutical habits and the proper use of critical tools, disciplines force inquirers to honor investigative routines more than the reality and individuality of the things seen. The rationality disciplines solicit leads to a mind-numbing, object-containing repetition of institutional knowledge. The coherence criterion disciplines uphold demands that results and conclusions be accommodated to established truths. The consequent homogeneity of concerns and behavior only impoverishes the world outside the library and the lab.

Because of its methodological basis, its satisfaction of interpretative policies, not the reality of things, "discipline" now stands for all the institutions of knowledge that compartmentalize the world and regulate the mentality of inquirers. "Discipline" has become a catch-all term for imperialism. It names any intellectual practice more concerned with preserving and imposing its own rules than with representing its objects. In current parlance, the feature that stands out most in a discipline's identity is its institutional inertia, the quotidian regularity that retards methodological change even when a new object or innovative inquiry renders a method obsolete. (Disciplines can accept new content, so long as their methods can assimilate it without self-revision.) "Discipline" means: "conservation of institution through the policing of disciplinary conduct." "Discipline" used to signify training, specialization, professional expertise, scholarly authority authenticated by already authenticated scholarly authorities. As such, "discipline" connoted trustworthy labor, reliable interpretation, normative inquiry. "Discipline" now signifies the same thing—training, etc.—but with contrary values attached to those significations. Disciplinarians are trained, but the training amounts to indoctrination. They become professionals, but their professionalism resides in their personal representation of a profession, not in their direct representation of the world. They have authority, but their authority comes at the cost of progressive thought.

This is to say that the professional meaning of discipline has evolved into a moral meaning. When one utters the word "disciplinary," a range of immoral associations follow: "repressive," "institutional," "misrepresentative," "judgmental." And because disciplinarity has no moral weapons to counter with—disciplines validated themselves not on moral but on pragmatic grounds—this means that disciplinarity is doomed. Its death certificate has been written by the master of disciplinary suspicion, Michel Foucault, who remarked in "The Discourse on Language,"

Disciplines constitute a system of control in the production of discourse, fixing its limits through the action of an identity taking the form of a permanent reactivation of the rules. (224)

As soon as discipline becomes a system of control, not of training, a scheme of indoctrination, not of education, a reactivation of rules, not a representation of the world, discipline falls into disgrace. Disciplinary scholars have no effective means of fending off this discredit, for they must admit that training is indeed a form of control, that disciplines do operate according to rules. Their excuse that disciplinary control is a useful thing, that rules have institutional benefits that are not preponderantly immoral, carries little weight in a moral climate where any kind of control is culpable. Disciplines are manifestations of institutionalized power, and power is bad. (For many, though simplistic, this is the lesson of Foucault's *Discipline and Punish*.)

The term "disciplinary" serves a defensive moral purpose in contemporary criticism. It frees inquirers from methodological restraints and shields them from methodological attack. Against the disapproval of those who insist on sufficient evidence, argument, and other research criteria, non-disciplinarians can file the charge of "disciplinarity" and rest content with having confounded their antagonists. Methodological observance is a symptom of institutional control, of professional investments, and "disciplinarity" sums up the attitude that buys into the institution. The utterance of the term in academic debate has the moral force to send opponents backpedaling.

discourse For a long time, the word "discourse" signified any more or less organized body of writings and utterances sharing a basic referent. Although linguists and semanticists developed a precise technical definition of the term, for most critics working in the humanities, "discourse" meant a referentially tied grouping of communications. "Humanist discourse" denoted texts and statements that described, posited, analyzed, and otherwise touched upon humanist principles and attitudes. "Biochemical discourse" named any language acknowledged as relevant to the field of biochemistry. The "discourse" side of the epithet signified a common content. The only complication of the term lay in whether the treatment of the content need be affirmative or not, as in the question of whether discourse containing anti-humanist statements counts as humanist discourse, in that it refers to humanism, or strictly as anti-humanist discourse, since it affirms only the opposite. But this ambivalence between a common referent merely referred to and one affirmatively referred to did not materially trouble the usage of "discourse." The meaning was plain enough.

Then came Michel Foucault. In his genealogies of asylums, prisons, disciplines, and sciences, Foucault gave to "discourse" an ominous and powerful new significance. Discourse was no longer a set of referentially similar statements. It was a historically developed and institutionally enacted mechanism of control geared to the production of putatively real and normal things like facts, rationality, and subjects. In Foucault's all-too-familiar understanding, discourse is a practice, not just a language, a practice involving the utterance of certain meanings *and* the constitution of an institutional field that admits those utterances. To the Foucault inquirer, any established discourse points to a set of discursive practices, which "are characterized by the delimitation of a field of objects, the definition of a legitimate perspective for the agent of knowledge, and the fixing of norms for the elaboration of concepts and theories" (*Language, Counter-Memory, Practice*, 199). "Discourse," then, while retaining its old meaning, now includes the grounds and contexts of a discourse's appearance, the delimitations, legitimations, and norm-fixations that enable it to stand as the regular language of a science, a discipline, a group, or a technology.

Discourse implies binding prescriptions and functional exclusions. No discourse exists in a social vacuum. It must compete for place, maintain its institutional warrant. The discourse of psychoanalysis, for instance, not only aims to analyze psyches. It also regulates its own field, identifies members and misusers of it, guards against interlopers bearing a non-psychoanalytical notion of psyche, an argument against the authority of the analyst, a different model of the analytic session, and other transgressive designs. With the modes of organization and legitimation that go into the establishment and maintenance of any discourse now added to the meaning of "discourse," with the exercise of power and adjudication now embedded in every exemplary utterance of a discourse, the term loses its abstract linguistic neutrality. Power relations, institutional police work, behavioral taboos, rites of authenticity, the production of normative knowledge, in sum, the sociopolitical realities of institutions, all are now implicated in "discourse."

Hence its appeal to literary and cultural critics today. The word "discourse" has a linguistic basis and so it seems well-suited to critics trained in the interpretation of language and rhetoric. After Foucault, discourse has a more than linguistic and formal purview. A discourse is a system of social control, an index of constitutive racial, sexual, sociopathic, and psychological distinctions. Therefore, in analyzing discourse, critics escape the academic seclusion of the formal, structural study of language and broach sociohistorical processes, many of which involve unjust but rationalized modes of oppression (such as the way seventeenth- and eighteenth-century discourses of rationality stigmatized madness). The representation mandate is fulfilled and the moral basis of criticism is secured, plus critics need not step outside their area of competence. They can analyze texts much as they did before, but now they can call it "discourse" and appear as more than textual explicators. They are henceforth cultural watchdogs, historical detectives, institutional diagnosticians.

In "Inventing a Feminist Discourse: Rhetoric and Resistance in Margaret Fuller's *Woman in the Nineteenth Century*," Annette Kolodny pushes the thesis that Fuller's writing style marks the advent of a political and cultural alternative to patriarchal ways of speaking. Fuller's treatise is characterized by a conversational rhetoric, one reflecting her own renowned powers of conversation and criticized in her own time for not obeying the conventions of writing. However, what contemporary male critics considered a stylistic failure is, in fact, the deliberate invention of a different discourse: "Fuller must be read on her own terms, and *Woman in the Nineteenth Century* must be accepted as an intentional experiment in a feminist discourse that refused premature closure" (379). The conversational mode is more than just a different rhetoric. It is a feminist discourse. With all the institutional associations hovering around the word "discourse," the choice of style here is elevated above the world of letters and made into a social declaration and a political commitment. Fuller's conversational writing is a compositional option *and* a cultural paradigm shift. That is Kolodny's claim and the conversion of "conversational style" into "feminist discourse" justifies it.

Another essay that takes "discourse" as a cultural strategy to be diagnosed, not a language to be analyzed, is Russell Reising's "Lionel Trilling, *The Liberal Imagination*, and the Emergence of the Cultural Discourse of Anti-Stalinism." Reising summarizes Trilling's early criticism and Cold War attitudes and argues that Stalin came to embody the "monolithic, reductive, ideological thinking and . . . simplistic politics that . . . Trilling spent his career attacking" (110). The funny thing about this essay is that, while it devotes many pages to citing historical evidence that calls anti-Stalinist discourse into question, it does not produce any specific examples of anti-Stalinist discourse. Reising indirectly refers to anti-Stalinist beliefs and McCarthyite behaviors (accusations of mass murder, torture, economic mismanagement, etc.), but he never provides any substantial samples of the language and communication—the discourse—they appeared in. One infers that "anti-Stalinist discourse" covers any statement critical of Stalin. The methodological advantage here is that in calling the statements "anti-Stalinist *discourse*," Reising can cast a daunting variety of historically compounded, ideologically twisted texts and utterances as a simple political tactic: discredit Stalin, promote the United States. The term "discourse" retains some vestige of linguistic meaning, but it has gathered enough political meaning (discourse as "geopolitical strategy") to render detailed linguistic analysis unnecessary.

This generalizing function serves well critics who write sentences like the following (all the italics are mine):

Scientific discourses are "lumpy"; they contain and enact condensed contestations for meanings and practices. (4)

The constructions of an organism's boundaries, the job of the *discourses of immunology*, are particularly potent mediators of the experiences of sickness and death for industrial and post-industrial people. (10)

At first glance, there is a limitation to using King's scheme, and that limitation is inherent in the "facticity" of *biological discourse*, which is absent from *literary discourse* and its knowledge claims. (11)

From the mid-twentieth century, *biomedical discourses* have been progressively organized around a very different set of technologies and practices. . . . (14)

Concurrently . . . the question of "differences" has destabilized *humanist discourses* of liberation based on a politics of identity and substantive unity. (14)

Race and sex, like individuals, are artifacts sustained or undermined by the *discursive nexus of knowledge and power.* (15)

These constructs may be conceived and built . . . in terms of complex, structurally embedded semiosis with many "generators of diversity" within a *counter-rationalist* (not irrationalist) or *hermeneutic/situationist/constructivist discourse* readily available within western science and philosophy. (16)

These sentences all come from one article, "The Biopolitics of Postmodern Bodies: Determinations of Self in Immune System Discourse," by Donna Haraway. Besides these sentences, the article also has references to "the plane of political and moral discourse usually suppressed in scientific writing" (17), "immune system discourse about the body's 'technology' for recognizing self and other" (17–18), "postmodern biotechnical, biomedical discourse" (18), "travel discourse" (25), "Expansionist western medical discourse" (28), "tones of colonial discourse" (29), "institutionalized discourses in medicine, war, and business" (30), "liberal discourse on the collective and personal individual" (30), "the abstract spaces of national discourse" (30), "emerging western and multicultural discourses on health, sickness, individuality, humanity, and death" (32), "modern western discourses" (39), and "biopolitical discourses of individuation" (40). That makes twenty-eight discourses in all.

Haraway does not specify the attributes of the discourses named (the discourse of one immunological text receives brief treatment). She invokes labels after offering scant evidence for them and then moves on. For example, "travel discourse" appears in the sentence, "This paper opened with a reminder that science has been a travel discourse, intimately implicated in the other great colonizing and liberatory readings and writings so basic to modern constitutions and dissolutions of the marked bodies of race, sex, and class" (25). On what does the "intimacy" imputation rest? On the fact that an immunology textbook couches the discovery of the suppressor T cell in the phrasing, "He thrilled at seeing the layer upon layer of that complexity which no one had seen before" (quoted on page 5), the latter phrase recalling the *Star Trek* line, "to go where no man has gone before." This, Haraway affirms, is proof that "Science remains an important genre of western exploration and travel literature" (5). It is part of travel discourse.

What is happening when a term proliferates like this, when it applies to so many different things but the application remains so distant and abstract, so feebly substantiated? To call science "travel discourse" but not to analyze it in detail as travel discourse serves no scholarly purposes. So why throw it around so loosely? Because it satisfies a representational purpose: it points toward the "condensed contestations for meanings and practices" (4), the construction and maintenance of institutional boundaries and normative subjective identities. The citation of the "discourse of *x*" is intended not to designate *x* and its verbal formulas, but to elicit the practices that structure and legitimate *x* as an authorized topic. "Discourse" usage names not an object, but an organizing process. Above, by calling science this or that discourse, the critic casts science as a disciplinary code, a social agenda, a juridical surveillance of persons. While non-discourse descriptions of a language simply detail its diction and grammar, discourse descriptions treat the language as a coercive socialization. The "discourse" label adds the element of power to the mores of communication and the elliptical reference to power relations counts more than the enumeration of verbal attributes.

But why leave the label so unsubstantiated? Why not document the genesis and pragmatics of the discourse cited? Because the very concept "discourse" will not itself be defined, will not submit to clear and precise predication. If definition and description are themselves modes of discourse, how can they present discourse as an object of definition and description? As Paul Bové argues in *Mastering Discourse: The Politics of Intellectual Culture*, "these essentialist, defining questions quite precisely *cannot* be asked of 'discourse'" (5). Definition and description are two of the subtlest versions of discursive practice, and hence "these essentializing questions emerge from the very interpretive models of thought which the new focus on 'discourse' as a material practice aims to examine and trace" (5). Attempts to define "discourse" will have to implement the very thing they propose to define—a question-begging impasse that leads to an infinite regress. "Discourse," then, remains in part indeterminate.

This explains the popularity of the term. It harbors moral uprightness and political incisiveness, but it does not isolate a concrete object. One can confidently cite "the discourse of x" and not feel obligated to fill out the citation with specifics. "Discourse" connotes institutional practices of exclusion and validation, but it does not denote a definite system of reference. The term has a loaded meaning, but a vague referent, and the vagueness is necessary to this mode of inquiry. In using it, critics can attenuate their descriptions, yet still sound authoritative. "Discourse" usage converts a methodological weakness into a theoretical exigency. "Discourse" is an essential constituent of inquiry, description, definition, and so an inquiry into any particular discourse must hold off from being too determinate, too positive. The ubiquitousness of discursive products (norms, values, distinctions, etc.) fosters a healthy skepticism toward the methods of empirical investigation (hypothesis testing, observation, factfinding). Hence critics can make incidental citations of this and that discourse, the mention of them indicating a world of relevant sociopolitical processes, and rightly neglect to fill in the concrete sociopolitical ingredients of the discourses cited. The meaning of "discourse" and the methodological evanescence of it vindicate empirical thinness and oblique statement.

essentialize Although the concepts "essence," "universal," and "nature" have remained at the center of Western philosophical discourse for over two thousand years, literary and cultural criticism has picked up the concepts in the last fifteen or so years and embraced them as if they constituted a recent and indisputable addition to knowledge. The concepts often appear in adjectival form ("essentialist," etc.) and get applied with the utmost confidence and self-satisfaction to a variety of intellectual attitudes. These ontological ideas are now seen as umbrella terms relevant to all beliefs in transhistorical properties. The detection of such ontological assumptions in any particular interpretation or school of thinking often counts as a subversion of the latter's legitimacy. Some usages even seem to imply that any implementation of absolute predicates or uncontingent subjects rightly suffers the charge of "universalism" or "essentialism," terms whose very utterance marks a decisive indictment.

Do these uses of ontological concepts and their classification as "essentialist" have any bearing upon Aristotle's definition of essence, Locke's distinction between "real" and "nominal" essences, or Husserl's search for the essence of consciousness? Rarely. Literary and cultural criticism's debates about essences, universals, and nature hardly ever invoke the concepts' philosophical background, nor do they propose to resolve philosophical questions of what essence is, where universals are to be found, how nature is to be distinguished. (Diana Fuss, quoted below, is a mild exception.) Whether because they consider the philosophical issues settled or simply because they are unaware of the philosophical tradition, critics apparently deem a philosophical rationale for their use of the term unnecessary. When using "essence," "universal," "nature," or any other "essentialism," critics for the most part have other goals in mind.

But what is the point of invoking the philosophical terms, if it is not a philosophical one? Why borrow concepts from ontology if not to make ontological inquiries? Perhaps one might say that it is not necessary to make ontological arguments every time we implement a concept derived from ontology. A concept can be lifted from one discipline without submitting it to that discipline's disciplinary uses. But can one borrow concepts from a discipline's conceptual field, place it in another, and ignore entirely the original context? What becomes of the meaning of ontological terms in critical discourse?

A clue to the strategic value of ontological references is that when they enter into critical discourse the terms usually assume a verbal form. One casually hears in academic debates today the phrases "such-and-such universalizes x," or "that idea rests upon a naturalizing of x," or simply "you are essentializing x." Here are some examples:

To be gay in this [judicial] system is to come under the radically overlapping aegises of a universalizing discourse of acts and at the same time of a minoritizing discourse of persons. (Sedgwick, "Across Gender, Across Sexuality: Willa Cather and Others," 60)

For [Henry Louis] Gates, the task of the Afro-American literary critic is, in part, to attend to the ways in which language (re)inscribes naturalizing or essentializing notions of "race." (Fuss, *Essentially Speaking*, 76)

By making explicit the cultural construction of racial subjectivity, Fanon de-essentializes both race and psychoanalytical models of subject formation. (Bergner, "Who Is That Masked Woman?" 76)

In each case, a long-standing and often controversial ontological concept is transformed from a noun into a verb. What does such a conversion entail?

Let us focus upon the latter example, "essentialize." The assertion is often presented as a refutation, as if its mention constituted a valid argument. In this usage, the point functions as an argumentative shortcut or rhetorical dismissal. What the gesture means is: "You are making x into an essence, into an immutable, natural quality that makes the thing it supposedly inheres in what it is." What is devastating about the statement is not its imputation of a supposedly objectionable ontological position to the other side. Wholly convinced of their own constructivist view, anti-essentialists consider an ontology that admits essences as patently false. Ontological grounds for affirming essences are simply unthinkable. So, rather than addressing the ontology of essentialism, the accusations imply or diagnose a political strategy at the root of essentialist thinking: the essentialized thing serves essentializers as an indisputable ground from which they can draw conclusions about the persons or things bearing that x as a property. That is, essentializers can make x into a defining attribute and then use it to justify certain social or political distinctions as stemming from natural distinctions. Essentialism, then, is an intellectual device concocted to naturalize and legitimate historical constructs, social hierarchies, political privileges. It poses an uncontingent, unchangeable, pre-human basis on which cultural differences properly rest. The phrase "You are essentializing x" acts to underscore this process, to expose a putatively given state of affairs as a human creation developing along the lines of group interests and identity politics.

We may admit the frequent usage of essences as political alibis for various repressions. But let us set aside the historical documentation necessary to support such a conclusion and instead examine the logical grammar of the phrase "so-and-so is essentializing x." First of all, does it even make sense to turn "essence" into a verb? If "essence" refers to some immutable, inherent, definitive quality of some object, can this quality be put in the object by some human act of essentializing? Of course not, for essence by definition cannot in actual fact rest upon a social construction or an interpreter's projection. If essences do exist, they pre-exist any individual human experience or invention. The process of their recognition works by logical derivation, not by an essentializing finagling. Again, by definition, essences are discovered (un-empirically), not invented. So, on the issue of essentialization being an untenable process, both sides agree: those who believe in essences say you cannot essential*ize* anything and those who disbelieve in essences say you cannot essentialize anything, if by "essentialize" we mean "to make into an essence."

Herein lies one rhetorical virtue of the verb "essentialize." The word sounds like a decisive injunction, a summary reckoning that forbids any rejoinder. It discounts the essentialist's agreement and disagreement. That is, the essentialist's disagreement—"No, I am not essentializing *x*"—almost appears to be a concession, a wholesale acknowledgment that any affirmation of essence is invalid, not to mention repressive. And the essentialist's agreement with the implicit premise—"Yes, one cannot really essentialize anything"— also appears to be a resolute capitulation to the anti-essentialist position. That is, the verb aligns the debate subtly but inalterably in favor of constructionism. If another verb were used, "impute," for example, then a genuine argument could proceed. If the anti-essentialist said, "You are imputing an essential nature to *x*," then one could respond either with "No, I am imputing an *accidental* nature to *x*" or with "No, I am *deducing* an essential nature from *x*." But the verb "essentialize" disallows any response from the start, and so the two sides do not, strictly speaking, even engage in logical dispute. Hence, the use of "essentialize" does not logically disprove essentialist arguments, but rhetorically silences them.

This is not to say that essences actually exist. The analysis only purports to show that the phrase "so-and-so is essentializing *x*" is a contradictory formulation if understood ontologically. To say that something is or can be essentialized is already to deny its essentiality. It is to transfer the ontological category of essence into a conceptual field—call it the "politics of interpretation"—in which the concept "essence" can have only a contradictory meaning. In such a framework where all ontological concepts are considered to owe their character to the political interests of their conceivers, "essence" refers not to the inherent whatness of a thing but to the political effects of the concept's use. That is to say, essence becomes an act, not a nature. Hence the verb, the "-ize."

However, given the traditional definition of "essence" as the permanent, non-accidental, and ultimate nature of a thing, essentializing is an act that is logically impossible. One might put the contradiction this way: the phrase "so-and-so is essentializing *x*" requires the ontological definition of "essence" in order to reject the definition. That is, it invokes the meaning of "essence" in order to deny that "essence" denotes any actual entity. What does it denote, then? If "essence" does not refer to any actual thing, quality, or attribute, what does it refer to? Well, again, when "essence" becomes a verb, that indicates that its reference to some real thing matters less than do the political causes and effects of the act of essentializing. Hence the anti-essentialist's role simply is to highlight essentialization as a discursive strategy. For him or her, essence is just one more intellectual power play, one particularly insidious because it strives to hide its political maneuverings. Essentialist thinking conceals its interestedness behind a rhetoric of universals and truth, rationality and logic, concepts supposedly depersonalizing and depoliticizing essentialist inquiry. This is the camouflage the anti-essentialist purports to discover. And he or she does so not by engaging oppositionally in debates over, say, the essence of the Good or the rationality of God's essence. Rather, the anti-essentialist rejects outright such ontological determinations and all the forms of assessment that go with them.

Again, since the concept "essence" entails such determinations, "essence" must have a new definition, a reference to a practice and not to an entity. Anti-essentialists shift the question from "What is essence?" to "How are essences produced and circulated?" Obviously, the latter essence is already understood to be a social formation, historically determined, while the former is a special category of being. So, while posing the second question, anti-essentialists cannot ask or answer the first question. The terms in each question have fundamentally different definitions; the one essence has little to do with the other. When anti-essentialists employ the phrase "so-and-so is essentializing *x*," they implicitly subordinate the ontological meaning to the discursive meaning—a logical confusion given the fact that ontology cannot be subordinated to discourse, but only redefined by it, displaced by it, ignored by it. In a universe of discourse and practice where a concept's meaning is inextricable from, if not identical to, the power relations the concept presupposes and sustains, particular inquiries always remain circumscribed by the institutional, ideological import of ontology as discourse, as a political practice. To take seriously any specific ontological conclusion, even the conclusion that "There are no essences," anti-essentialists would have to suspend the discursive, political context. But because of that context's foundational status in anti-essentialist criticism, such a withholding is impossible. Indeed, the very use of the verb form "essentialize" forbids it. But this is precisely the advantage of the "-ize" tense. Though the accusation has no empirical or logical meaning, it does trap essentialists into accepting the discursive meaning of the term—a winning rhetorical play.

gender   In *Gender and the Politics of History*, Joan Wallach Scott has a concise chapter on the semantics and uses of the word "gender." In assessing how gender serves as "A Useful Category of Historical Analysis" (the chapter's title), Scott begins by exploring the different meanings of the term and the roles they play in various schools of thought. Scott notes that "feminists have begun to use 'gender' as a way of referring to the social organization of the relationship between the sexes" (28). These feminists emphasized the social dimension because they "wanted to insist on the fundamentally social quality of distinctions based on sex" (29). "Gender" signals an assertion that inequalities between men and women were socially derived, not biologically determined.

Scott then mentions a related usage of "gender" designed to curb a one-sided focus on women in women's studies scholarship. This usage strove to "introduce a relational notion into our analytic vocabulary. According to this view, women and men were defined in terms of one another, and no understanding of either could be achieved by entirely separate study" (29). This meaning of gender was intended to correct the excesses of a fledgling field of inquiry (women's studies) trying to establish its legitimacy and its discrete and proper compass.

Next, Scott says "'gender' was a term offered by those who claimed that women's scholarship would fundamentally transform disciplinary paradigms" (29). Because the study of women would not only "add new subject matter but would also force a critical examination of the premises and standards of existing scholarly work" (29), the analysis of gender would enact redefinitions of history and society, develop new concepts, distinctions, and syntheses upon which disciplinary work is based. As historians developed the concept "gender," other concepts and concomitant methods would follow, and so the field would change. Since existing historical premises could not adequately account for gender (and had perhaps repressed it), new premises would have to arise and with them a new disciplinary practice.

This methodological turn leads Scott to consider a variety of theoretical understandings of "gender." First, the "simplest recent usage," is when "'gender' is a synonym for 'women'" (31). Scholars substitute "gender" for "women" in titles and summations in part to grant legitimacy to their field, to make their work sound less partisan and more serious. Because "'gender' has a more neutral and objective sound than does 'women,'" it escapes "the (supposedly strident) politics and feminism" and joins the social sciences as an intellectual inquiry free of bias. Also, the "gender" for "women" exchange "explicitly rejects biological explanations" (32). "Gender" here underscores the constructedness of male-female distinctions and opens an area of investigation that differentiates "sexual practice from the social roles assigned to women and men" (32).

This meaning of "gender" applies to relations between the sexes and, in doing so, it provides a descriptive tool for historical study. However, the substitution meaning does not reveal why male-female relations are the way they are, only that they are social and that inquirers can recount the course of their socialization. In order for "gender" to assist in the analysis, not just description, of social formations, it must have a meaning and a method that is useful as a theoretical tool. The theoretical meaning of "gender" is provided, Scott says, by three major critical approaches:

The first, an entirely feminist effort, attempts to explain the origins of patriarchy. The second locates itself within a Marxian tradition and seeks there an accommodation with feminist critiques. The third, fundamentally divided between French post-structuralist and Anglo-American object-relations theorists, draws on these different schools of psychoanalysis to explain the production and reproduction of the subject's gendered identity. (33)

Scott proceeds to outline each approach in several lengthy paragraphs. The first effort addresses the general subordination of women and uses "gender" to reveal the ideologies patriarchy concocts to justify or naturalize that subordination. The second effort brings gender issues into the socioeconomic sphere and assumes that sexual divisions of labor are not due to the exigencies of biology. "Gender" in this Marxian perspective highlights the gender component of many aspects of capitalism (but does not forsake a materialist basis for either gender or capital). The third effort proposes a concept of gender based on psychoanalytic notions of identity formation, language being the matter out of which gender identity is constructed (38). "Gender" in this approach serves to loosen the rigidity with which the processes of identity construction contain subjects.

Each of these methods of gender definition and analysis is inadequate, Scott argues. They either fail to historicize gender appropriately (as in the way psychoanalysis locates all gender questions in an individual subject) or to theorize gender appropriately (as in descriptive history's superficial narrative of gender relations). To overcome both drawbacks, Scott proposes a better definition of gender, one with "two parts and several subsets":

The core of the definition rests on an integral connection between two propositions: gender is a constitutive element of social relationships based on perceived differences between the sexes, and gender is a primary way of signifying relationships of power. (42)

Gender is a mode of constitution and means of signification, the former of social relations and the latter of power relations. These are abstract formulations in need of clarification and so Scott attaches to the first "four interrelated elements" (43): one, "culturally available symbols that evoke multiple . . . representations—Eve and Mary as symbols of woman, for example, in the Western Christian tradition—but also, myths of light and dark, purification and pollution" (43); two, "normative concepts that set forth interpretations of the meaning of the symbols" (43), doctrines that contain their metaphoric possibilities; three, "a notion of politics and reference to social institutions and organizations" (43) such as labor markets and education; and four, a historical concept of "subjective identity" (44), one which places subjective identity into "historically specific cultural representations" (44). These four elements "clarify and specify how one needs to think about the effect of gender in social and institutional relationships" (44).

As for the second proposition—gender as the signification of power—it may seem to imply that gender operates as a normative concept (number 2 above), but in fact gender functions at a more basic level than that of explicit doctrine. When fulfilling a semiotic function, "Established as an objective set of references, concepts of gender structure perception and the concrete and symbolic organization of all social life" (45). Here, gender is not an object of social beliefs and mores, but a basic determinant of them. Even perception has its gender factor. In places where gender does not seem to function ("war, diplomacy, and high politics"—48), the hierarchical structures that do function often have implicit gender distinctions as part of their organization. This is why theoretical gender "provides a way to decode meaning and to understand the complex connections among various forms of human interaction" (46). All forms of political power are articulated through explicit and implicit gender categories— "Political history has, in a sense, been enacted on the field of gender" (49)—and so gender analysis reaches into spheres seemingly devoid of gender, but in truth structured by gender. "Gender" here is a revelatory mechanism. Once the concept "gender" enters into historical scholarship, the tacit gender relations underlying seemingly non-gendered power relations come to light.

Scott's complicated definition of "gender," with its propositions and subsets and its multiple historical-theoretical sides, reveals how dense and critical the term has become in contemporary scholarship. (Scott's layout has been influential enough for Louis Montrose in "The Work of Gender and the Discourse of Discovery" to take it as "a theoretical groundplot for the particular historical and critical, local and individual concerns of the present essay"—2.) On Scott's composite analytical model, "gender" has an elaborate historical bearing (on symbols, myths, concepts, doctrine, organizations, and subjectivity) and an omnipresent theoretical pertinence (wherever relationships of power are articulated). It informs large-scale political groupings and reaches into personal psyches. It directs the tacit understandings of nature and society, the common but unconscious theoretical knowhow through which individuals order the world and make it meaningful (see Scott, 2). Gender is not only a marker of sexual difference. It is a strategy of differentiation in general, explicitly a sexual one, but implicitly a social, political, and economic one. Scott's definition and consequent methodology of "gender" is lucid and effective because it delineates a historical concept and procedure of recuperating differentiated "femininities" *and* it uses theoretical tools that delve into the differentiations' implicit regions. Gender as a historical tool recovers historical information and processes. Gender as a theoretical maneuver penetrates the ideological, pseudo-natural disguises that sublimated the information and processes.

This dual perspicacity of "gender" so conceived suits well the purposes of literary and cultural criticism. Although critics usually eschew the historiographical labor that Scott's definition obliges researchers to carry out, the synthesis of historical and theoretical allows for a happy combination of empirical description and general statement. This is often just the kind of unity critics desire, especially when they wish to derive broad cultural conclusions from their interpretation of a minute set of texts. If gender is both an empirical fact and a constitutive mechanism, if gendered phenomena incorporate objects and their gendering, then a discussion of gender in this or that text can slide smoothly from the small detail to the broad generality. The trace of gender here or there signifies the work of gender everywhere. A particular object with obvious gender features is but one manifestation of a subliminal gendering operative throughout the cultural field the object belongs to.

This connection of particular and general has tantalizing methodological benefits for textual analysts. It makes every textual item with gender traits an instance, a heavily overdetermined symptom of a larger condition. With each singular specimen bearing the pressure of representing a widespread state of affairs, it is up to the critic to relieve that pressure through a close examination of the object's empirical facets and a consequent theoretical expansion of the object to general status. The "gender" citation facilitates that translation. An instance has a gender, has masculine or feminine characteristics—that is an observable fact. But "gender" is not only a quality, but a qualification. It is an attribute that imports a heavy cultural, social, and political load and does so subliminally—that is a theoretical supposition. So, a gendered moment in a text marks a determinate situation, a logic, an ideology, a framework, or a consensus that includes gender as one of its functional constituents. Within that space of overdetermination, the critic has room to speculate, to fulfill his or her job of interpretation. The critic can enumerate the gender circumstances of the text—a sound practice, but by itself an unsatisfying one for most critics— and then extend the inquiry to the general outlines (cultural, political, sexual) vaguely indicated by the local circumstances.

Thus, in "The Somagrams of Gertrude Stein," Catherine R. Stimpson quickly surveys different representations of Stein's body by herself and her acquaintances only to conclude that "Stein's texts, including her somagrams, warn us against going on to genderize grammar itself" (42). Stimpson has said nothing up to this point about grammar per se, but she has discussed Stein's "coding of sexual activities" (39) and others' descriptions of her "unfeminine" body. The reference to gender allows for the leap from gender-laden writings about Stein's body to the gender of grammar, of language itself. Gendered as it is, Stein's experimental writing becomes an "anti-language" belonging to an "anti-society," one formed on a principle of homosexuality.

The expansion of local detail into universal condition through "gender" citation also works in Susan Wolfson's "*Lyrical Ballads* and the Language of (Men) Feeling: Writing Women's Voices." There, Wolfson notes the gender ambiguities in Wordsworth's *Lyrical Ballads*—where Wordsworth speaks in a woman's voice or gives to male characters "motherly" sensibilities, but also has male characters express shame for such emotional weaknesses—and then refers to this as a "poetics of gender." We move from a gender variation among characters, an empirically observable fact, to a poetics of gender variation, a theoretical construct from which the variations follow. From gendered statements by and descriptions of Leonard, Michael, the balladeer, Harry Gill, and other Wordsworth characters, which Wolfson scrupulously catalogues, we derive the implicit principle of Wordsworth's theory and practice of poetry.

Here and elsewhere, "gender" functions as a methodological translation. In "Mama's Baby, Papa's Maybe: An American Grammar Book," Hortense Spillers moves from an intricate reading of the maternal situations in *Narrative of the Life of Frederick Douglass, Autobiography of Malcolm X, Incidents in the Life of a Slave Girl*, and "The Moynahan Report" to a summary statement about feminist and cultural discourse. She writes: "Because African-American women experienced uncertainty regarding their infants' lives in the historic situation [slavery, poverty, patriarchy], gendering . . . *insinuates* an implicit and unresolved puzzle both within current feminist discourse *and* within those discursive communities that investigate the entire problematics of culture" (78). The horrible circumstances of maternity for African-American women (for example, a slavemaster taking their infants away from them) yield a key to understanding women and society. One particular gendered situation reveals an "entire problematics of culture." A daring interpretative leap, yes, but justified by the insertion of "gendering," for gender is "an *outcome* of certain political, socio-cultural empowerment within the context of the United States" (77).

D. A. Miller works a similar translation of local explication into broad application in his interpretation of *The Woman in White*. After noting how some male characters in the novel suffer from nervousness and that "nervousness is always gendered in the novel as . . . an 'essentially feminine malady' " (190), Miller concludes that a violation of "gender identification" has occurred. The characters try to contain their nervousness, but their efforts only "produce further evidence of the gender slippage" (191). Given the fact that the novel, as a suspenseful mystery and a "Victorian sensation novel," also causes the reader to feel nervous, Miller can say that "Every reader is consequently implied to be a version or extension of the Woman in White" (191). As readers caught up in the fiction, "we 'catch' sensation from the neuropathic body of the Woman who . . . is free to make our bodies resonate with—like—hers" (191). Miller draws this conclusion through the technique of "gender" generalization. Through the "gender slippage," a few characters' nervousness becomes *every* reader's implication in neurasthenic confusions.

This is the methodological function of "gender" in much criticism today: to expand textual interpretations into cultural summations. "Gender" facilitates the jump from particular to general. With "gender" functioning as both an attribute and an "outcome," the logical problems of drawing general conclusions from a scant sample of particulars are obviated. The normal requirements of probable inference do not obtain. Even when admitting the tenuousness of cultural generalization from a few textual examples, critics can call upon "gender" to ease the transition. When Rita Felski asks, "What is the gender of modernity? How can anything as abstract as a historical period have a sex?" the answer is simple: "Gen-

der affects not just the factual content of historical knowledge . . .
but also the philosophical assumptions underlying our interpretations of the nature and meaning of social process" (*Gender of
Modernity*, 1). Hence, every historical period necessarily has a gender and every object in that period that has a gender in some way
represents the gender of the period as a whole. Gender is both accidental and constitutive. As such, it is a remarkably useful instrument of criticism, especially when criticism wants to extend textual
analysis to social, political, and cultural commentary.

ideology   "Ideology" as a critical term dates back to Marx and
Friedrich Engels, who define it in *The German Ideology* as "the ideal
expression of the dominant material relationships, the dominant
material relationships grasped as ideas" (136–37). Marx and Engels have precursors and followers who use the term in a slightly
different sense, and Marx and Engels themselves sometimes conceive "ideology" in a neutral way as the ideas representative of a
class and its interests, but overall the rationalization-of-privilege
meaning is the most prevalent one in current parlance, although
the type of privilege is not always class-based. (See Raymond Williams's entry on "ideology" in *Keywords* for a neat intellectual
history of the term. See the opening chapter of Terry Eagleton's
Ideology: An Introduction for a broad discussion of the term's meaning in contemporary political thought.) Critics speak of "bourgeois
ideology," "the ideology of modernism," "Enlightenment ideology," and so on with the firm understanding that the designations refer to a system of ideas and representations that correlates
with social distinctions and political-economic structures. "Ideology" adds a material component to concepts, puts intellectual
labels like "Enlightenment ideas" into contexts of class struggle,
group justifications, identity politics, and naturalizing strategies
whereby humanly invented ideas acquire a seemingly given existence and sanction.

Ideological analysis, then, entails a dogged empirical accounting
of the material conditions (labor relations, land distribution, racial
demographics, etc.) that parallel the "mental production" (Marx)
of culture. A relentless dissection of ideology as opposed to an
exclusive focus on ideas, concepts, truths, and other abstractions
counteracts the tendency toward idealization, keeps the concrete
circumstances of intellectual practice from disappearing in the

mists of philosophy and aesthetics. Obviously, such a vigilant inclusion of social determinants in the analysis of texts and ideas
appeals to critics who feel anxious to tell the social truth. A concentration on ideology reverses the elitist academic habit of forsak-
ing concrete working conditions and group interests and studying
ideas and texts in their abstract purity—to many critics, *the* crime
of New Criticism, structuralism, deconstruction, and other formal-
isms. When struggling against such separations of mental and material, ideological analysis has a counterideological end: to expose
the rationalizations that intellectuals and other stewards of culture
concoct for dominant groups.

Ideology further appeals to critics because the ideologies intellectuals serve up to an epoch are, to an extent, embraced uncon-
sciously by those living in that epoch, including the intellectuals
themselves. To them, the system of ideas that has been removed
from its worldly conditions seems to exist apart from those conditions. In the course of this intellectual evolution, ideological critics
contend, ideology no longer stands as a set of discrete ideas explicitly decided upon, but as a framework of basic assumptions within
which individuals think. That is how it is experienced. Nobody ever
sees its creation. Nobody even cognizes it, much less chooses it. A
prevailing ideology mingles with the natural world and becomes
part of it. Ideology and forgetfulness go hand in hand. Except for
ideological critics, that is, who become diligent guardsmen in the
struggle against this ideological oblivion.

This is a personal advantage of the "ideology" citation. It casts
those who subscribe to an ideology as blind and deluded (Marx
and Engels often call ideology an "illusion"), as complacent and
unwitting accomplices of various social and political structures
that support their intellectual privilege. Intellectuals', artists', and
professors' ideologies are too implicit to be recognized clearly, too
rationalized to be singled out, too comforting to be rejected. Only
ideological critics can do that. The leaders and representatives of
the intellectual circles, who are the unconscious representatives
of dominant economic forces, announce their ideology as a discovery, a philosophy, a method, and a science to a credulous world
and everyone believes it, including the intellectuals themselves.
But, in truth, they know not what they do. Their intellectual inventions emerge from an ideological framework that they remain
incognizant of.

One can sense that condescending judgment about ideological blindness in sentences like the following:

An important formal feature of horror fictions, then, would seem to be the inducement and subsequent disguise of audience identification, and what might be called the film's [*The Silence of the Lambs*] manifest ideology serves to redirect attention away from powerful lines of identification that thereby remain latent. (Elmer and Wolfe, 142)

If we see history only in the narratives it produces, and if those narratives are unconscious ideologies, then ideologies will have narrative structures that are politically charged. (Loesberg, 116)

The presumptuousness of these statements lies in the imputations of unconscious control that ideology exercises upon those experiencing it. People watch movies and take in their ideology without realizing it. People read history without sensing the ideology enacted in it. Even when ideology becomes "manifest," Elmer and Wolfe say, it does so only as a feint, to make "powerful lines of identification" become hidden to those doing the identifying. Ideology is a background phenomenon, a functional set of distinctions and associations crucial to the cognition of social reality, but ever receding from individuals' attention. It is "politically charged," Loesberg says, but strategically subtle. Ideology is a universal fugitive, at work everywhere but recognized nowhere. Only the ideologically wary critic knows its machinations.

Occasionally, ideological blindness extends even to critics themselves. In "The Harmony of the Tea Table: Gender and Ideology in the Piano Nocturne," Jeffrey Kallberg observes that music historians shy away from gender "because the idea that instrumental music occupies an autonomous realm still remains a powerful ideological force in the discipline. Those of us who would seek to lessen the stranglehold of this ideology on modern critical discourse encounter particular difficulties" (102). Note the movement here: from an idea that instrumental music is autonomous to a full-blown ideology of autonomy. An idea espoused becomes an ideology enforced. Music critics do not simply believe, among other things, that instrumental music is to a degree independent of social and political contexts. Critics embrace a thoroughgoing system of interpretative presuppositions and practices that center upon the proposition of autonomy, and this system "strangles" non-autonomy-based approaches to music. Those music critics who disclaim the autonomy assumption become outlaws of their own discipline. A basic disagreement with one formalist principle turns into a benighted rebellion against institutional repression.

Another example of how "ideology" approaches exalt the critic at the expense of mere experiencers and narrow disciplinarians is Charles Bernheimer's "Degas's Brothels: Voyeurism and Ideology." Bernheimer's essay proposes to analyze Degas's paintings of prostitutes and dancers and to determine how the paintings situate male viewers socially, psychosexually, and, ultimately, ideologically. However, in ideological terms, the thesis of the essay never pans out, for Bernheimer never specifies what ideology is at work in the Degas setting, nor what material conditions correspond to it. In fact, he spends little time discussing ideology at all. In a few paragraphs near the end, Bernheimer mentions four ostensibly related ideologies: "capitalist ideology that defines and confines woman's value in representational practice," "hegemonic ideology based on sexual counterphobia," "patriarchal ideology," and "misogynistic ideology" (176–77). This is a weighty mingling of economic, psychological, anthropological, and social variants, and one expects a discrimination of them to follow. But Bernheimer does not bother to clarify the denominations. He casually drops the names and moves on to other points. So why make the references?

"Ideology" appears a few times elsewhere in the essay, but not in order to finger an ideological structure. Instead, Bernheimer uses "ideology" to characterize the attitude of the viewer of Degas's paintings. He writes of the "ideological assumptions underlying his voyeuristic position" (160), of "the suspect ideological artifice of that construction" (160), of "the way ideology abstracts the individual and asserts power through invisibility and absence" (174). These allusions indicate the function "ideology" performs in the argument. Bernheimer does not cite "ideology" in order to isolate a set of ideas and assumptions serving as the intellectual counterpart to a concrete social, political, or economic condition (as in Marx). If that were the case, Bernheimer would spend more time enumerating the specific contents of the ideologies he so blithely names. The point would be to document an idea as part of an ideological network and then connect that network to specific socio-politico-economic practices. But here the assertions point to an individual's experience, not to a cluster of materially based ideas. Bernheimer's "ideology" statements insert the ideological network into the interpreting mind of the onlooker. An individual looks at Degas's painting of naked prostitutes sitting on a bench waiting for clients and sees it through an ideological "artifice," an "underlying," "suspect," "invisible and absent" mental filter. The subject observes the painting, and the observation becomes an index of ideological pressures and commitments proper to the subject's culture and class.

"Ideology" assertions thus distinguish two attitudes to objects, the consumer's and the critic's. The consumer takes in the object through ideological eyeglasses, interpreting it through a set of subliminal dispositions molded by social and political interests. The critic takes in the object *and* the consumer's ideological vision. He recognizes the limitation of consumption to the "artifice," knows the "invisible" ideological content "underlying" the surface particularities of the object. (Oftentimes, the creator of the object will be unaware of the latent ideological meaning and become a fool of ideology.) In referring to an ideological dimension of objects and experiences, the critic opens an interpretative space for herself. Between herself and the consumer, between the manifest text and the latent text, lies an area of interpretation that only ideological critics can work upon, bring to light, criticize in order to underscore the processes by which ideological assumptions get inscribed upon seemingly non-ideological materials.

Bernheimer's citations of ideology serve less referential purposes than they do rhetorical purposes. He has no interest in detailing "capitalist ideology that defines and confines woman's value." His interests lie in differentiating one interpretative approach from another and asserting one's superiority. The "ideology" citation empowers his own critical perspective, both cognitively and politically. Cognitively speaking, putatively non-ideological attitudes are blindly ideological, and those who embrace them become suspect, though unconscious participants in a cultural concealment. Ideological concerns render a previously obscured region of inquiry— the ideological backing—open to critical inspection. Critics now think ideology, not just assimilate it. Politically speaking, ideological criticism has a keener understanding of political processes and their multifarious disguises. Ideological critics will not be duped, will not give in to intellectual seductions. They keep their glance fixed on the material grounds of ideas and methods and on the ideological basis of objects and behaviors. Although ideology is everywhere and even informs their own criticism (as they reiterate), their heightened awareness makes them less guilty of complicity. The "ideology" usage certifies this cognitive discernment and political resistance.

-ing One often finds this verb form in titles of scholarly studies ("Opening Up the Canon," "Writing Women and Space," "Redrawing the Boundaries") and in seminars and conferences ("Mapping and Remapping the Disciplines," "Theorizing the Body"). But despite the popularity of the present progressive tense in criticism, the purposes it serves remain methodologically troublesome. Obviously, the tense calls attention to the act, to the operations described, not just to its outcomes. Whether it refers to an action on the part of the critics themselves or of the objects or persons studied, the "-ing" form signals an ongoing social or institutional process, a still unfolding change in the cultural geography. The "-ing" tense also affirms the scholars' participation in that process, their involvement being either a watchful documentation of the cultural changes or an active reconstitution of their own work. That is, when talking about "Reviewing Sex," "Defining Southern Literature," "Questioning Romanticism," "Economizing America: Virginia Farmer, Tuskegee Student" (by Mark Bauerlein), or "Reclaiming Rhetorica: Women and the Rhetorical Tradition," critics mingle their subjects' transformative gestures with their own revisionary criticism. For example, the title "Defining Southern Literature" names two complementary critical procedures: Southern writers define and redefine Southern literature and Southern scholars do the same in an evolving constitution of literary culture. The "-ing" usage spotlights this mutual involvement, emphasizes the scholars' role in it, keeps it moving and guarantees its salubrious progress.

This is the first institutional boon of the "-ing" usage: it satisfies critics' narcissism. The critical process, singled out by the "-ing" verb, receives such mindful scrutiny because, to put it bluntly, critics in process crave recognition. They want their efforts to matter, to have cultural capital. So, scholars focus on their own critical acts to dignify those acts, to validate them as a worthy object of critical attention. If critics just did their work and produced a result, the result would enter an impersonal arena of disciplinary debate and only indirectly endow critics with value. But if critics add their own energies to the topic of discussion, they draw themselves into disciplinary conversations. If they talk about "theorizing *x*" instead of actually developing a theory of *x*, critics authorize themselves as theorists. If they concentrate on "questioning *x*" instead of posing questions of *x* and answering them, critics exhibit themselves as unrelenting interrogators. While it is true that in the evaluation of scholarly work, the results of an inquiry count more than does the inquiry's genesis, the appreciation of inquirers themselves calls for an open display of the critic at work. If a group of scholars come together to "remap the disciplines," their new map is pragmatically more important than the ways they went about doing the remapping. The result of their endeavors has clear methodological value, for scholars can take the new map and build a discipline of criticism and teaching within it. Personally, however, the mapping is more important, for a successful map only exalts the critics as mappers, not as persons. The story of the endeavor itself has a biographical value, one exceeding the disciplinary identity of the critic. The critic becomes important as a person.

This narcissistic interpretation of the "-ing" usage speaks to the desire of academic critics to collar social prestige, but it shortchanges another, non-personal motive for the "-ing" usage. For, besides the hankering for personal standing, there is also a methodological reason for critics' diligent awareness of their own institutional acts. The argument runs: the more explicit scholars are about what they do, the more they save themselves from unwittingly fostering institutional structures and effects that they themselves oppose. When scholars begin "remapping the curriculum," they call attention to their own ways and means of remapping in order to ensure that their implicit critical habits do not counter the very curricular changes the scholars wish to bring about. A relentless audit of the critical process rebuffs any methods that might subvert the end of that process. A keen attentiveness to critical gestures keeps critics sensitive to the contexts of inquiry, the politics of interpretation, the mores of scholarly activity. Power operates through institutions in subtle sublimated ways, and only a penitent consciousness of assumptions and consequences can keep critics from doing interpretative wrongs to their subjects.

However, though it may justify self-consciousness as a provisional critical attitude, this semi-methodological, semi-political rationale for "-ing" and other calls for attention is inadequate to explain the perpetuation of self-consciousness. Self-scrutiny as a safeguard against critical abuses does not fully account for why criticism must remain so ceaselessly focused on its processes, not its products. For, one assumes, the purpose of such self-exposition is to certify the products, not to underscore the product-making. One brings to light one's tacit assumptions and hidden supports only in order to flesh out their political and moral influences. One examines one's methods in order to confirm their consistency and practicality. Once critics pose those questions and the contexts and premises pass the political, moral, and methodological tests, critics may return to their productions confident of their propriety. In the remapping instance, once we have inspected our remapping assumptions and methods and determined their legitimacy, we need no longer inspect them nor need we hearken to our remapping conduct. We have satisfactorily reviewed our grounds and procedures and we may now develop more ideas, distinctions, and information from them, not re-examine our implementation of them. We might ask whether the remappers begin with true premises and clear goals, whether they draw conclusions logically, whether they handle their concepts and data deliberately, and so on. But if the remapping follows valid methods, then we may safely proceed to examine the consequences of the remapping, namely, the new map.

Beyond the determination of the remappers' methodological soundness, what interest can the actual process of remapping have for scholars and teachers who wish genuinely to modify their practices? In so far as the endeavor serves as a valid example of how desirable and pragmatic remappings should be carried out, it deserves attention. But if the actual remapping is the important thing, if the "-ing" mode prevails for other than exemplary purposes, does that mean that scholars should merely continue the remapping process, perform it again and again? What else can they do with the remapping action? If they wish to evaluate it, then they will have to characterize their labor as "evaluating the remapping," a perspective that then calls for "evaluating evaluating the remapping" and so on. If scholars decide upon a non-stop inquisition of their own critical processes, if they insist upon a present progressive observance of themselves at work, then they turn critical practice into a hyper-self-critical meta-method, an enervated inquiry whose object is the rather uninteresting spectacle of interpreters interpreting.

The insufficiency of critical self-consciousness to justify the present progressive usage does not mean the usage is wrong, but only that it needs further warrant from other quarters. That warrant may be found in yet another semi-methodological principle, what we might label "the principle of ongoing interpretation." This idea rests on the proposition that an emphasis on the product of interpretation entails a false hypostatization of critical inquiry. Inquiry is a fluid behavior, a changing concrete practice, and any attitude that abstracts a result from the conditions of its advent distorts the result's merely relative stability. While set definitions, regular methods, and empirical data fossilize interpreter and interpreted into static polar entities fixed in their categorical positions, the present progressive tense explodes that reification and remains faithful to inquiry's dynamic character. Though an inquiry's conclusions often provide useful information and effective models, that detachable outcome compromises the truly ongoing nature of interpretation and reality. Although some measure of abstraction and stability must take place in order for an inquiry to carry over to others' scholarship and to the classroom, such institutional exigencies do not alter the fact that culture and history are evolving wholes, that contingencies come and go, that critical interests change. True, for a reading of a text, a conceptual invention, or a mode of analysis to have institutional longevity, for scholars to import it into their own work and for teachers to pass it on to students, that intellectual event must assume a transmissible, economical, objectified state. But once that process crystallizes into definable concepts, conventional truths, and established methods, inquirers have abandoned their fidelity to historical process. The concise, communicable form of non-progressive tenses (not "remapping the curriculum," but "we have remapped the curriculum") marks a false stasis, a pat conclusion easy to use but untrue to the realities of change.

The present progressive tense and other action-oriented gestures reconnect criticism to historical process. Though ongoing inquiry forestalls its own use, it does present inquirers with an accurate representation of how interpretations and their objects develop. And it grants to other critics more than just an observer role. Once scholarship becomes a critical process paralleling historical change, scholars and teachers are welcome to join in the critical procession, to start "-ing"-ing themselves. (This explains the often collective nature of "-ing" inquiry. For example, of the nineteen book listings for "rereading" in the MLA Bibliography, 1981–95, seven are edited collections.) Everyone from professors to students may see himself or herself as an agent of scholarly change, a generator of critical activity, an academic mind ever in flux. All critical inquiry will become processual and all critics legitimately involved in the process. The results of any single inquiry will matter less than critics' participation in a general unfolding academic enterprise. Logical and formal evaluation of any single interpretation will become untenable, since the only way one can apply those criteria is to step outside the process and apply fixed standards to it—a spurious claim.

These, then, are the current merits of the "-ing" usage: 1) it spotlights the critics; 2) it guards against thoughtless complicity with institutional power; and 3) it ties critics to historical change.

interdisciplinary The term "interdisciplinary" has such critical currency today, serves so many diverse rhetorical and argumentative designs, means so many different things to different people, that a competent semantic discussion of it is impossible in a glossary entry. Apart from the referential variations of "interdisciplinary," the pragmatics of the word involves a legion of psychopolitical overtones, personal resentments, hermeneutical suspicions, honorific pretensions, moral wrath, and self-congratulatory sentiments that only a full-length institutional diagnosis could adequately detail. Leaving that task to institutional historians, I will present a set of illustrative usages of "interdisciplinary" in order to demonstrate the heterogeneous meanings of the term. Instead of taking the following citations as an epitome of how "interdisciplinary" functions in critical discourse, consider them a partial inventory of the term's divergent and tenuously related references.

The project of the cultural studies of science is not to announce the arrival of interdisciplinarity; it is to help us find our way in a world that is always already interdisciplinary. (274)

In the prehistory of feminist cultural studies . . . there stand two monumental studies, Virginia Woolf's *A Room of One's Own* and Simone de Beauvoir's *The Second Sex*, both models of original inquiry into the female condition and of interdisciplinary approaches to that inquiry. (277)

To the extent that literary criticism has concerned itself with reference, it has had an interdisciplinary object. . . . The assumption that words *mean* is itself interdisciplinary. (280)

Perhaps it is more useful, therefore, to regard interdisciplinarity as the normal condition of intellectual progression. (285)

My various interdisciplinary and multicultural projects have made me feel that I am creating new knowledge rather than merely passing knowledge on, which latter approach conservatives seem to honor exclusively these days. (295)

Many forms of literary and cultural studies are, of course, intrinsically interdisciplinary by drawing from several distinct disciplines . . . but the distinction of interdisciplinary studies has less to do with a centripetal drawing together of particular, related disciplines than with centrifugal, polytropic proclivities. (308)

These citations are all taken from a 1996 Forum in *PMLA* on interdisciplinarity. The authors are, respectively, Alan Rauch, Lillian S. Robinson, Mark Schoenfield and Valerie Traub, Derek Attridge, John Lowe, and David Graver. In each one, "interdisciplinary" refers to something different. In the first, the term predicates "a world" and signifies the world's diverse make-up. A world is "interdisciplinary," the statement argues, because it exceeds any disciplinary approach, any "artificial notion of mutually exclusive categories" (274). But if disciplines break up a world into categories, do interdisciplines *not* break up a world into categories? Epistemologically speaking, can any glance upon a world, disciplinary, interdisciplinary, or merely live, not focus on a part of it? The attribution of "interdisciplinarity" to a world here begs those questions. All we have is the assertion that "interdisciplinarity" yields a more adequate representation of the world.

In the second quotation, the term refers to two books and signifies the books' diversity of discourses. The first book, Woolf's great feminist pamphlet, includes several non-literary "alien tongues, including the discourses of history, economics, and sociology" (277), and so it counts as interdisciplinary. I doubt an economist would agree that *A Room of One's Own* constitutes economics; that a work contains language that is part of a discipline's jargon does not qualify that work as disciplinary. But here it does. "Interdisciplinary" means simply "mingling of discourses."

The third example attributes "interdisciplinarity" to an interest in reference and an assumption that words mean. Because words mean through "the meaning-producing movement that occurs *through* the frames of disciplinarity" (281), as in the way "marriage" in a Shakespeare sonnet "draws its meaning from discourses of history, religion, and heterosexuality" (281), meaning is itself an interdisciplinary construct. Which is to say, all speaking animals are unconscious interdisciplinarians, for the assumption that words mean is not a conscious choice, but a tacit component of any communication. "Interdisciplinarity," then, forms the basis of meaning, intelligibility, rationality. Without interdisciplinarity, nothing makes sense.

The next citation treats "interdisciplinarity" as "the normal condition of intellectual progression." Interdisciplinarity is a process of creative intellectual labor, of the production of new knowledges and innovative practices. Disciplines crystallize those productions into "various types of consolidation, such as pedagogy, popularization, political organization, the formation of identities, and the establishment of institutions" (285). Interdisciplinary thinking confronts those disciplinary formations as they settle into routine achievements. Interdisciplinarity breaks down well-worn institutional boundaries, takes liberties with the script of disciplinary rehearsals. And it revises disciplinary structures in order to propose better disciplinary structures, for the "consolidation" of interdisciplinary inventions into institutional forms is the normal course of "intellectual progression." "Interdisciplinarity" here signifies the imaginative part of a circular process of the creation and destruction of intellectual systems.

The following quotation relates "interdisciplinarity" to the professor's generative capacities. (This personal reference seems inappropriate to a general discussion of interdisciplinarity in literary studies, but strangely enough, thirty-one of the forty-two Forum responses involve personal description and anecdote.) By being interdisciplinary, scholars and teachers create new knowledge, not just pass on old knowledge. They become epistemological inventors, not just traditional transmitters. Interdisciplinarity is the way thinkers break free of epistemic paradigms, imagine alternative cognitive attitudes, impart revisionary wisdom to students and readers. Interdisciplinarity transforms the professor, liberates him or her from the conservations of the past. The term here signifies a pedagogic leap, an endowment of conceptual originality. The professor is now an academic prophet.

The last quotation begins with a straightforward definition of "interdisciplinary": work "drawing from several distinct disciplines."

But the sentence quickly turns on its head. Interdisciplinarity draws disciplines together, but, moreover, it disperses its own activities in "polytropic ways." It does not unify disciplines into a monolithic field of study, but rather incorporates them and implements them in sundry and manifold directions. Here "interdisciplinary" signifies an integrative-disseminative process, a method that is catholic but not universal, diffuse but not incoherent.

These are some of the usages of the term "interdisciplinarity." It can signify a diverse world, a work of prose, communication, normal intellection, a professor's originality, or a centripetal-centrifugal proclivity. One might argue that these usages do not explain anything about interdisciplinarity as a matter of "inter-"ing disciplines. One might expect interdisciplinary thinking to devote itself to developing focused "inter-" methodologies that do more than juxtapose contents from different disciplines. If "interdisciplinary" means not just a casual sharing of disciplinary materials, if it names a cogent integration of concepts, methods, and aims, then interdisciplinary proposals must provide a methodological framework that genuinely synthesizes disciplinarily discrete materials. Sanguine pronouncements about "collaborative work," "global awareness," "bridging the disciplinary gaps," "forging new institutional linkages," and the like are insufficient, just as is a professor's training in one discipline and dabbling in another.

But these are complicated professional issues skirted by the usages above. If the usages typify the meaning of "interdisciplinary," then the term applies not to a unifying method, but to texts, worlds, institutions, and professors. Although its connotations remain roughly the same—"counterinstitutional," "diverse," "liberal," "progressive"—its denotations vary from utterance to utterance, that semantic variety being held to be a signature of intellectual imagination. If the term "interdisciplinary" ever settled into a new method, firmly established and institutionally recognized, these multiple personal, political, worldly, and professional references would subside. Critics and teachers would have to relinquish the rhetorical-institutional gymnastics of the term "interdisciplinary" and carry out the normal travail of founding an academic inquiry.

literary criticism   At the risk of banality, one might answer the question "What is literary criticism?" by saying, "Literary criticism is the criticism of literature." It is not criticism of history, economics, sociology, or any other disciplinary subject matter. To ask "What is literary criticism?" then, is to beg the question "What is literature?" That question invites the supposition that a text either is or is not literary, that it does or does not contain some quality, element, or essence of "literariness." But what if a historian comes along, reads an acknowledged piece of literature such as Mark Twain's *Pudd'nhead Wilson*, and interprets it as a fictional representation of 1890s racist anxiety over the legal status of black citizens and the social status of mulattoes? His criticism begins on the assumption that Twain's story translates contemporary historical conditions into plot and character. His criticism ends when he has translated Twain's narrative of Dawson's Landing into an historian's account of steady legislation against and disenfranchisement of African-Americans in the post-Reconstruction era, that historical phenomenon being fictionalized by the novel. In doing so, the historian removes those formal and rhetorical complications that most literary critics claim constitute the literary qualities of the text. Literature here is fictional representation of history, the conversion of historical fact into the narration and characterization specific to *Pudd'nhead Wilson*. It is up to the historian to return those novelistic particulars to their real world antecedent, to extrapolate from them a historical condition and then lay them aside.

This is an admittedly caricatured description of how a good historian reads literature. But even in this form, the historian's interpretation can stand up to the question of whether it has overlooked or violated something in the text. The answer is that, of course, it has done so, and has done so precisely to do something else. The historian's goal is to draw historical conclusions from the novel, not to pose literary, philosophical, or other non-historical questions about it. The more the interpretation raises literary questions like "How does *Pudd'nhead Wilson*'s satire resemble Swift's satire?" or philosophical questions like "What is the status of personal identity in the novel?" the less it answers historical questions about the novel. The more the novel becomes a literary or philosophical object, the more it assumes the form of literary tropes or philosophical propositions, the less it will be a historical representation and admit to historical interpretation. One might regard this interpretative variance as a difficult hermeneutical problem, but more simply it stands as a methodological circumstance. The novel can be many things and one of its determining factors is inter-

preters' presuppositions and designs. This is not to say that interpreters cannot see any other possibilities for the novel, but only
that in order to explore one possibility consistently and deeply,
interpreters remain as a matter of choice roughly within one understanding of the novel and in the methods that go with that
understanding. The historian brackets non-historical approaches
to the text for pragmatic reasons, to make the historical interpretation more economical and direct. The historian does not want
extrahistorical concepts and strategies to cloud his or her dealings
with the work. So, from the very start, the historian reads the text
as an indirect record of history, uses it to draw historical conclusions or to complement historical evidence. In his or her hands,
that is what the text is. That is how it works. To the literary critic
who says, "But you read only a part of the text," the historian re-
plies, "And you don't? Can you or anyone read the whole text, in
all possible ways? Do I want or need to do anything different with it
than treat it historically? Am I competent to do otherwise?"

The historian studies the historical features of narrative and the
literary critic studies the literary aspects of language. Cultural and
political critics are bound to condemn that concept of literary criticism for being too narrow and formal, for being disciplinary and
apolitical. But they cannot condemn on methodological grounds
the practice of defining literature as forms of language having characteristics of x, y, and z and then doing formal analyses of x, y, and
z as they appear in this or that work of literature. For this is a pro-
cedural issue, not an evaluative one. If we accept a definition of
literature as, say, organic form, we do not then censure critics
who study literature in non-organic ways. When they skip formal
analysis and instead situate literature historically or extrapolate
a politics from it, critics do not get literature wrong. By not heed-
ing this methodological precept, they simply no longer do literary
criticism.

The point is that the historian reads the text historically, the sociologist sociologically, the philosopher philosophically, the literary critic literarily. Their identity as such lies precisely in their
competence to carry out their appropriate interpretative activities.
Inquirers begin with a concept of the object, of its meaning and
nature, and their methods follow accordingly. As soon as an inquirer approaches the object from one disciplinary standpoint, the
other standpoints are largely foreclosed. For the concepts and

practices making up the respective approaches constitute a methodological framework that has its own internal coherence and does not easily admit to revision by or mixing with other frameworks. The relations that structure a framework do not take shape haphazardly. The conceptual and methodological relations that hold various definitions, postulates, and practices together in a framework like that of historical inquiry give to its constituents a form of logical and pragmatic affinity with one another. Historiographical concepts and practices make up a complex that has its own integrity, its own logical and methodological structure. Introducing a philosophical understanding of a concept like "representation" (and the philosophical mode of analysis that goes with it) into the historiographical complex shakes up the historiographical complex and confuses historical interpretation.

Of course, because of all the historical and institutional meanings encoded in any text, and because of those meanings' affiliations with interpreters' historical conditioning, the text's receptivity to disciplinary approaches will vary. A historicist reading of a Wallace Stevens poem would probably produce less significant results than would a phenomenological reading. But then a historicist reading would likely work better on an Honoré de Balzac novel than on a Stéphane Mallarmé lyric. We may assign those differences to convention and not to the object itself, but in actual practice, they nevertheless mark resistances "in" the object and prevent any single disciplinary approach from submitting the *entire* object to its interpretative grasp. A disciplinary approach cannot as if by fiat transform an object into a pure disciplinary construct and eradicate all attributes that do not fit the disciplinary conception. A phenomenological analysis of a song by Whitman explores the intentional acts of consciousness in the poem, but it says nothing about the typeface, pagination, and bookbinding of a particular edition of *Leaves of Grass*. And yet, to a textual editor, such material facts are crucial to a scholarly understanding of Whitman's work. In either case and in general, something of the object remains beyond any particular methodological approach. But this is not cause for dismay. Rather, it is cause for accepting the fact that, from an absolute perspective, inquiry works more as a matter of attention and inattention, with a scholar focusing on those attributes that meet his or her disciplinary identifications and ignoring those that do not. Interpretation involves the object's material features and historical meanings and the interpreter's disciplinary background (which selects only some of those features and meanings for description). As for the interpreter's own historical circumstances, one purpose of disciplinary training is to subordinate the interpreter's social, political, and personal singularities to a systematic and communicable method of inquiry. Disciplinary training, in part, is devoted to making a person's interpretative acts into consistent procedures that can be recognized and evaluated in some standard way. This is what method does: it organizes the historical, structural, social, and political variables in the object and in the interpreter into a workable, transmissible activity. Indeed, without some form of methodological simplification, organized inquiry could not proceed. Texts, persons, and events, with all their causes and circumstances, are simply too complex to allow for exhaustive, impartial interpretations, interpretations that do not narrow the field of inquiry down to practical limits. These are artificial delimitations, to be sure, but they are necessary for inquiry to function in an institutional setting. Partiality per se is no drawback of any interpretation, and a method that selects one portion of a phenomenon for study has no basis for assessing a method that selects another portion of it. The relative value of an interpretation rests not upon its superiority to an interpretation coming from another disciplinary perspective, but upon how superior it is to other interpretations coming out of the same perspective.

In short, an interpretation's merit depends upon how well it fulfills its own disciplinary aims. You cannot compare interpretations from different disciplines, for there is no common standard to evaluate them by. Strictly speaking, though they address the same text, they approach it with such different premises and designs that the text they practice their interpretations upon differs from discipline to discipline. Or rather, none of these interpretations has any way of getting around the literary text, the historical text, or the otherwise disciplined text to reach the text itself. The methodological assumptions of each discipline lead the historian, the literary critic, the anthropologist, and so on each to select from the text different aspects of it for study.

This is not to say there is no such thing as *the* text. The assertion of there being different texts does not indicate some deep hermeneutical truth, but only a methodological fact. Interpretative practices follow from different concerns, perspectives, and methods and the latter yield different versions of the same text. To do, say, a literary interpretation, a critic must read *Pudd'nhead Wilson* not as a text but as a literary text, just as a historian reads it as a historical text. However the text actually exists before the interpretation takes place, a reader's disciplinary premises will specialize it. In its particular interpretative acts, a literary analysis does not proceed by at first reading aimlessly and then discovering a general literariness in the text. It assumes a general literariness and then describes the specific literary aspects peculiar to that text, that the text uniquely bears out. Likewise, a historical interpretation assumes a general historicality in the text. To drop those kinds of assumptions and look at the text itself may or may not be possible, but even in the former case, dropping the general assumption means one is no longer doing a systematic disciplinary interpretation. This is why interpretations from different disciplines are incomparable. One can compare different assumptions, but not the interpretations arising out of those respective assumptions.

One might add that, not contradicting one another, interpretations that occupy different disciplinary frameworks and have different methods and purposes need not cancel one another out, for they can certainly coexist fruitfully. Whether that disciplinary framework is at bottom a conceptual framework, a linguistic framework, or an ideological framework, it constitutes a methodological barrier that prevents the concomitant interpretations from being placed into logical relations of contradiction, correspondence, similarity, and so on. Now, certainly, some texts put pressure on the methodological exactitude optimistically suggested in the above paragraph. If we are to understand a novel like *Robinson Crusoe* satisfactorily, then we must bring some economic analysis to bear upon the plot and setting. The economic situation of the novel, plus the tradition of economic commentary upon it, is too prominent for non-economic interpreters to ignore. But such problematic cases, with their demand for a less partial approach, may be settled pragmatically, by provisionally revising our distinctions and methods and retaining open confidence that the revision need not be wholesale, but should be localized as much as possible. This is not to say that literary study cannot learn from, borrow from, or be corrected by non-literary study and vice versa. Disciplines certainly affect one another, but these effects, when they have a local application, can only add material to an interpretation, not correct it. If one discipline wants to correct another, it can only do so by applying to the other discipline as a whole, to its foundational principles, not to particular examples of that discipline. For example, if a historian criticized a formalist literary reading of *Pudd'nhead Wilson* for ignoring the historical content of the novel, this criticism would not apply so much to that individual reading of *Pudd'nhead Wilson* as it would to formalist readings in general. That is, the historian's attack would pertain to any discipline that embraced formalist interpretation, and the formalist analysis of *Pudd'nhead Wilson* would come under attack only in so far as it was an instance of that discipline. Its clarity, cogency, penetration, and so on, would remain unexamined unless the historian could get beyond the historicist objection. This is why a particular literary interpretation can be evaluated only on literary critical principles. Only when a literary interpretation does historical work, drawing historical conclusions or implementing historical evidence, can a historical evaluation bear upon it.

Hence one interpretation cannot verify or falsify another from a different discipline. Scholars from different disciplines cannot compare who gets the text right, who is more true to it, for they each from the very beginning deal with different abstractions from the text. They start out with different assumptions about representation, language, content, form, and meaning and so they read the same texts differently. And the respective definitions of history, literature, sociology, and so on which inform those assumptions are not right or wrong. The ensuing descriptions can be right or wrong, but only in comparison to other descriptions that emerge out of the same definitions. There *are* false interpretations, but they are false only in relation to the disciplinary framework they emerge from. A formalist reading can read a poem wrong only formally. Historians read historically and their work can be judged in relation to other historical descriptions. But a historical and a formalist description cannot be compared without bringing terms to bear upon them that are not part of the conceptual field and terminology proper to those descriptions.

But what does it mean to read the text as literature? To repeat: What is literature? Wherein lies this fugitive "literariness"? What does "literary criticism" mean? Again, one might risk another simplistic answer. One does literary criticism when one postulates certain linguistic characteristics as literary and then analyzes those characteristics as they are played out, structured, developed, and so on, in various writings. "Literariness" is not a real entity. It is a disciplinary hypothesis. It says, "These qualities or effects are literary, and where we find them we are dealing with literature." To the extent the text has those characteristics, whatever they may be, it is literary. To the extent the critical analysis focuses upon those characteristics, it is literary criticism. (See John Ellis, *The Theory of Literary Criticism: A Logical Analysis*, pp. 24–53, for a discussion of this means of defining "literature" and various alternatives to it.)

To take a familiar example: the New Critics' formalist approach to literary language. Many scholars have sought to explain the advent of New Criticism by making large, vague, indiscriminate political generalizations about its origins. One often reads statements like "This movement [of New Criticism] responded to the complex forces of democratization transforming the educational institution" (John Guillory, "Canon," 246; Guillory's discussion of New Criticism in *Cultural Capital* is much more substantive). Since such summations are usually sparsely supported by concrete historical data, their accuracy remains undecided. Obviously, many historical forces went into the making of New Criticism. But while the big historical causes may reveal much about New Criticism as a historical phenomenon, they only indirectly explain the specific concepts and methods of New Criticism. If we wish to learn how and why New Criticism developed its theory of literature and practice of literary analysis, we need to examine exactly what problems and conditions the New Critics expressly wanted their definition of literature to solve. One of many specific reasons the New Critics evolved a theory of literature was a pedagogical one: teachers often claimed that they observed too many students of literature not reading with an attention to what many teachers considered were the proper literary elements in poetry and fiction. I. A. Richards's examples in *Practical Criticism* demonstrated that many readers of poetry generally opted to translate poetic language into feelings, ideas, or motives and to neglect the specific linguistic and literary basis of feelings, ideas, and motives as they were contextualized in the work. To inculcate a sensitivity to poetic language, Richards and, later, William Empson, Cleanth Brooks, W. K. Wimsatt, and others had to come up with a concept of poetic language that would compel students to avoid that translation, that would distinguish poetic language from non-poetic language ("scientific language," "denotative language," "prose") so that students could remain attentive to it. What they came up with, to put it simply, was that identifying poetic language rested on a semantic division between language easily paraphrased into abstractions, concepts, or feelings and language that resisted translation, that insisted somehow on its unique verbal form. The linguistic characteristics that countered the transparency of "prose," that complicated the extraction of content (feelings, ideas, motives, and so on) from language, were variously "irony," "ambiguity," "paradox," "contraries," "spatial form," and so on. After the New Critics isolated these literary features, literary criticism then had its discrete subject matter (every discipline needs its own proper object of study) and its legitimate practice (analyzing the workings of the above characteristics in individual poems by John Donne, John Keats, Gerard Manley Hopkins, and others).

Although New Critical methods of explication remain basic to the training of undergraduates in literary interpretation, the limitations of New Critical distinctions are fairly obvious to critics today: one, they fail to work satisfactorily in analyses of certain forms of fiction; two, the Critics sometimes tend toward an unqualified ahistoricism; and three, their distinction overlooks too many works that might be usefully considered literature. But despite those problems, New Criticism is exemplary in the way it developed a method of literary study. It offers a set of semantic attributes as literary and then reads texts and determines the presence and nature of those attributes in them. The definition of "literary" is a postulate, not a description, a methodological proposal, not a statement of fact. The primary thing is not its truth, but its workability, the extent to which it effects useful inquiry. Of course, in New Criticism, not every instance of irony, ambiguity, and so on is a *significant* piece of literary language. Only those writings that "contain" these semantic complexities in a closed system of literary-linguistic relations, a "verbal icon," a "well-wrought urn," merit extensive literary criticism. ("Form" here means "structure of meanings," not length of verse line, stanza form, or generic structure; see Brooks, 195.) If one adds this concept of totalized structure to that of semantic complexity, one can enter a New Critical framework and smoothly commence the practice. Again, this is not to hold up New Critical practice and its normative canon as exemplary. It is to hold up the New Critics' process of defining literature and literary criticism as exemplary. The resulting definition has its limits, limits we may find socially or politically unacceptable, but not because they are limits per se. Any definition must pose limits for it to have any determinate form and application. The question is whether those particular limits have value or not, which is not a literary question but an ethical, institutional, or pragmatic question.

The fundamental limit the New Critics establish is that between literary and non-literary language. Without this boundary, New Criticism as a whole remains imprecise and indistinct, an ill-defined discipline with no proper field of study. Indeed, one can extend this conclusion to literary criticism as a whole: unless a distinction is to be made between literary and non-literary, then literary criticism as such has no meaning. Why is this so? Because, as a principle of logic, the greater extension a concept has, the less meaning it has. If there is no division between literary and non-literary, then the predicate "literary" could apply everywhere or nowhere (and there would be no way of deciding which). In either case, in no way could it serve to direct criticism toward this text and not toward that text, toward one as significantly literary and another as not. Without the distinction, literary critics have no criterion to invoke when deciding which texts are and are not literary and why. This does not mean the criterion must be essential and absolute. It could be wholly institutional and conventional. One might say that "literariness" is not some essential semantic feature of literary language, but rather that it is a cultural practice of labeling some works of language "literature" and others not or of responding to some works in a certain way and others not and the labelling or responding rests not upon a linguistic reality, but simply on a cultural tradition. But though an essentialist criterion is not necessary, some criterion is. What the criterion must do is provide critics a means of answering the practical question of whether this or that language offers material for substantial literary analysis, whether literary methodology can work upon it in useful fashion.

But before that can happen, literary criticism needs the literary-nonliterary distinction to found its assumption, to give critical inquiry something to look for and other things to ignore. Whatever its origins and genesis, one thing the distinction does is provide a suitable workspace for literary criticism, support a disciplinary boundary literature departments might observe if they wish to differentiate themselves from history departments, sociology departments, and so on. The literary distinction supplies a disciplinary distinction, a basis upon which literary critics can do something that historians, sociologists, anthropologists, and others do not.

This fragmentation of knowledge into disciplinary divisions is precisely why the term "literary criticism" has become depreciative. With virtual unanimity, critics refuse to characterize themselves as merely "literary." Even a project like *The Johns Hopkins Guide to Literary Theory and Criticism* takes pains to ward off the suggestion that literary criticism is a discrete field of study. Rather, "literary theory always bears the impress of larger political and cultural debates," for "the boundaries of critical theory and practice are particularly permeable to influences from other disciplines and cultural hegemonies" (Macksey, v); "The disciplinary boundaries of the empire of criticism have always been notoriously unstable" (v); literary criticism connects with "underlying social, historical, or ideological interests and presuppositions" and borrows from discourses that "extend well beyond literature" (Groden and Kreiswirth, ix). Such cautionary notes against literary criticism's insularity, announced in a reference book, evince the decline of literary criticism as an organized field. Literary criticism has fallen into disrepute because its methodological prerequisite—a literary-nonliterary distinction— is a disciplinary invention whose only justification is its institutional effect: the organization of a discipline of literary criticism. It has no basis in nature and its only basis in culture lies in academic structures. Founded upon nonrepresentational axioms like "plot [is] a narrative of events with an emphasis on causality" (Prince, 72), literary criticism is an intellectual construct. The inquiry-creating process outlined above operates on pragmatic principles and institutional exclusions, not on the realities of history and culture. Executing a set of instrumental postulates ("literature is . . . ," "irony is . . . ," etc.), not representations of history, literary criticism strives for an internal coherence that subordinates the worldly involvements political and cultural critics promote. The methodologically based establishment of literary criticism says nothing about the contexts and complicities of the practice. Once critics accept the pragmatic model of literary criticism, they work within it, addressing samples of this or that literary abstraction in this or that piece of writing.

For these reasons, the term "literary criticism" now connotes an exemplary strategy of institutional construction antithetical to the demands of political awareness and cultural engagement. The methodological orderliness that makes literary criticism into a self-contained inquiry is the very thing that condemns it in contemporary debate. The boundaries and distinctions of literary criticism that seem useful and advisory are seen as repressive and bureaucratic. Pragmatic definitions of literature that open a discrete region of analysis become exercises in territorialism. Under this transvaluation of disciplinary values, the term "literary criticism" has become a rebuke of institutional sins.

the logic of   It is odd that, though criticism has routinely called into question positivist, empirical, and logical protocols of inquiry, the word "logic" frequently pops up in contemporary critical writings. Apparently, despite its associations with abstract formal analysis, with a philosophical tradition reaching from Gottlob Frege to W. V. O. Quine that literary and cultural criticism have found uncongenial, logic seems to bear some authority or cachet that critics consider desirable. One often finds epithets like "class logic," "cultural logic," "spatial logic," and "patriarchal logic" or the phrase "the logic of" functioning as organizing codewords in a critic's interpretation. The MLA Bibliography lists 492 scholarly books and articles published during the last fifteen years that have "logic" in their titles, a large portion of which are works of literary or cultural criticism. Two of the best-known critical studies of the last ten years propose to make an "-ism's" logic the focus of their speculations: Walter Benn Michaels's *The Gold Standard and the Logic of Naturalism* and Fredric Jameson's *Postmodernism, or, The Cultural Logic of Late Capitalism* (winner of the MLA's 1990 James Russell Lowell prize). Given the prestige and influence of such treatises and the sheer number of critical interpretations employing the "logic of" formula, it would seem that extrapolating a "logic" from literary and/or sociohistorical materials is an accepted and significant critical practice.

Here are some sample titles:

"Bodies of Terror: Theses Toward a Logic of Violence"
"Cultural Relativism and the Logic of Language"
Heuretics: The Logic of Invention
"The Logic of Ionesco's *The Lesson*"
"The Logic of Metamorphosis in Thoreau"

"The Logic of Modernism"
"The Logic of Realism: A Hegelian Approach"
"The Logic of the Reception of Céline's Works in the Thirties"
"The Logic of the Symbol"
"The Logic of the Undecidable: An Interview with René Girard"
The Logic of Writing and the Organization of Society
"Melville's Cognitive Style: The Logic of *Moby-Dick*"
"Reopening the Mysteries: Colonialist Logic and Cultural Difference in *The Moonstone* and *The Horse Latitudes*"
"Salvation History, Poetic Form, and the Logic of Time in Milton's Nativity Ode"
"Satire and Conversation: The Logic of Interpretation"
"The Sentimental Logic of Wollstonecraft's Prose"
The Social Logic of Space
"Wanting Paul de Man: A Critique of the 'Logic' of New Historicism in American Studies"

Of course, "logic" in these works of criticism means something much different from what Aristotle, William of Ockham, or Bertrand Russell mean by "logic." A target of study, not a method, criticism's "logic" has nothing to do with the structure of the syllogism, the principle of parsimony, or set theory. More broadly, criticism's logic says nothing about nor does it borrow from the rules of necessary and probable inference. It offers little in the way of clarifying relations between propositions as such. Rather, "logic of *x*" in the language of criticism signifies roughly the "inner workings of *x*," the latter phrase denoting either 1) the operative textual machinery of objects and discourses, or 2) the determinate historical unfolding of an ideology through objects and/or discourses.

As a dynamic textual structure, "logic" is synonymous with the system of differences, equivalences, and oppositions informing a text. As in Freud's "dream-logic," wherein a dream is the product of distortions, substitutions, and condensations that follow a determinate order unique to every psyche, "textual logic" is the sum of the above-noted relations that delimits the values, conceptions, and predications that make up the constituents of a discourse. For example, the "logic" of postbellum racist novels may be composed of the suppositions "whiteness marks superiority," "blackness equals subhumanity," "manual labor is dehumanizing," "virginity is an

unmarried white woman's highest virtue," and so on, all in determinate relations with one another. When these postulates become
activated in this or that novel, its plot and characters appear as
inevitable instantiations of that general racist logic. The novel's
course follows necessarily from its basic principles, and every character marks an affirmative or negative representation of them. If a
character violates a fundamental rule of racist logic, then the logic
demands that the plot must somehow eradicate or discredit him or
her. However, this logic is not to be confused with the cause-effect
relations of the story events. The logic pursued here is a "logic of
narrativity"—not the empirical causality of an event in the plot, but
the logical causality of the novel's entire emplotment. The critic's
task is to decipher that fundamental logic and apply it as an explanatory tool to other works falling in the same racist novel category.

On the other hand, as a historical process, "logic" is synonymous
with the ideological structure of x (the definitions, concepts, values, etc. of x) as it is manifested in texts, events, and other objects
as historical phenomena. That is, "logic" is not only x's ideological
structure but also the ways in which that abstract formation becomes materialized, and the materialization is just as foundational
as the ideology. To give the ideological structure a priority to or
privilege over the material instance, so the argument goes, is to
lapse into an ideology of structure itself, a tendency to assume a
transcendent structure from which all homologous raw materials
descend. To avoid that false disjunction, when referring to "the
logic of x," ideo-logic critics search out an active, complex system
of ideas, relations, and forms in historical process, while trying to
avoid either a materialist or an idealist preference. These identifications allow for a rational reconstruction of the historical record,
not a mere chronological account of what happened and when but
an interpretation of why it happened and why it had to happen the
way it did. The critic's task is to isolate these laws from their particular instantiation and apply them as explanatory tools to related historical facts.

These are the two meanings of "logic of" references and the
two interpretative strategies each respectively implies. Obviously,
whether identified with a textual structure or a historical process,
the significance of "logic" in literary and cultural criticism bears
little resemblance to the significance of "logic" in the work traditionally done by logicians. However, that does not mean critical

logic has no philosophical precedent. It only means that if one wished to outline a tradition supporting criticism's usage, one would ignore George Boole, Alfred Tarski, Donald Davidson, et al. and instead focus on Hegel and then pick up Freud, Heidegger, Derrida, and other Continental dialecticians. Criticism's logic of textual and historical processes derives from an intellectual genealogy that from the very beginning historicizes or textualizes logic. In Hegel's connection of every cognition with a phenomenology of mind, a mindset whose fundamental attitudes and organizing preconceptions are determinate and functional enough to produce that and only that cognition and thereby constitute an "epistemic logic"; in Derrida's "logic of the supplement," whereby representation turns upon a supplementary logic revealing the incapacity of the thing represented to stand for itself and the necessity of a representative to complete the represented; in Baudrillard's outline of the cultural class logic operative in a consumer society, whereby the use value of objects and of human needs gives way to a more basic set of rules and relations of exchange, prestige, and recognition, rules definitive enough to approximate a social logic—here and elsewhere critics may find "logic" consistently denoting the inner workings conditioning a way of thinking, a representational structure, or a historical process. Even though the Hegelian tradition has not made logic a distinct theme—how could it when dialectical thinking automatically rejects or complicates logic's foundational principle of identity?—it has provided critics with a more or less agreed upon reference. Specifically, for inquirers working in the Continental way, "logic" signifies a structure of differences, a network of terms unfolding in and through dialectical process. Even though classical logicians have judged the logic of Hegelian logic by and large utterly illogical, critics have found in Hegelian analysis a more or less consistent usage that openly eschews the binarism and linearity of Aristotelian logic.

But although the meaning of "logic" may be in one philosophical tradition sufficiently established as "inner determinants of a text or process," the citation of the term remains unfinished unless a methodology ensues that specifies what characteristics this or that logic has. If "logic of" appears in the title of some scholarly work, then a method of inquiry must follow that delineates what those determinants are and how they interrelate. If the logic refers to, say, a constellation of ideas and judgments at work in a gothic novel, then a correlative methodology of idea derivation from novelistic material is required. If the logic refers to the ideology at work in the operations of a racist culture, then a correlative methodology of ideology extraction from historical material is required. When one summons up a "logic of dissent," a "logic of *Ulysses*," or a "logic of the gaze," readers may understand the abstract meaning of the word "logic," namely, the active structuring mechanisms of a phenomenon. But the goal of the reference remains unfulfilled until the argument identifies the concrete logical particulars of the individual phenomenon and demonstrates how they add up to a logic.

In current critical practice the argumentation that purports to elucidate the nature and contents of the logic under scrutiny rarely supplies the information or reasoning requisite to a satisfactory description. Instead of presenting a large body of historical evidence from which one might infer a logic of one kind of cultural production, instead of developing a group of demonstrably true premises from which one might deduce a founding conceptual matrix, a logic of one kind of textual production, critics usually provide a commentary that is either empirically thin or logically slipshod. Ostensibly, when a critic refers to a "logic of *x*," he commits himself to an analysis designed to give to historical logics historical specificity and to textual logics structural precision. The aim is to distinguish the logic *as* a logic and *from* other logics, and only a meticulous enumeration of its historical and textual parts can do that. But instead of that process, today the rule of "logic" interpretation is scant empirical evidence for historical workings and sketchy conceptual analysis of textual workings. Critics cite the term as if it sufficiently indicated the contents of what it refers to, as if it were familiar enough to need no elaboration. Let us consider two prominent examples of "logic of" practice, the first employing logic as textual workings, the second as historical workings.

When Marjorie Garber broaches the logic of the transvestite, she neither compiles an inventory of conceptual or discursive entities making up the logic nor does she outline the determinate structure of them ("The Logic of the Transvestite: *The Roaring Girl* [1608]"). Indeed, her essay hardly even mentions the word "logic": we have only two casual references to "dream-logic" (228) and a quick reference to "the play's logic" (229). The sentence the first reference appears in runs: "The figure of the transvestite, in dream-logic already a figure *for*—as well as *of*—overdetermination, here becomes split into the apparently marginal and separable, and the apparently central" (227–28). What is this invocation of a "dream-logic" supposed to explain? In its standard psychoanalytic meaning, "dream-logic" signifies alogical acts of association and substitution whose manifestation in dream-work is determined, or "overdetermined," by unconscious forces. In a dream-logic context, then, the transvestite is both a function *of* repressions, condensations, distortions, and so on and a general metaphor *for* the way those psychic processes dovetail onto a single object.

Since the essay derives this transvestite dream-logic from no particular dream, the dream-logic noted here must come from the play itself and its representations of cross-dressing. But Garber supplies no evidence or argument demonstrating *The Roaring Girl*'s status as a dream-text. She refers at one point to the play's "unconscious"—"What else is in the play's unconscious? What does it know?" (223)—but this remarkable attribution of a psychodynamic to the play remains entirely unsupported. Garber leads up to this characterization with a paragraph on cross-dressing disguises and sexual innuendoes in the play, all of which, she asserts accurately, add up to a "homoerotic subtext." This subtext is "intrinsic to the inner dynamics of the play," the latter being precisely the play's "unconscious." But the leap from subtext to unconscious, even through these unspecified "inner dynamics," requires much more backing than a series of sexual metaphors and gender confusions provides. A subtext is a collection of tacit representations in a text connected by some thematic or figurative motif. An unconscious is a gathering of instincts and their vicissitudes. Or, granting the unconscious is in some way a text, it is a structure of differences, valences, and cathexes suffused with psychic energy, enduring in desire-driven restlessness, their mutual determinations becoming manifest in a variety of psychopathological behaviors. Until Garber proves that the subtextual elements fall into such a determinate, differential economy of psychic forces, the assertion that the play has an unconscious remains a hollow one.

Instead of presenting evidence or premises demonstrating the play's "unconsciousness," Garber opts for an argument from authority. She quotes from Lacan, original analyst of the unconscious structured as a language, extrapolating from his elliptical utterances about identity, language, and the phallus a "profound connection between theatricality and sexuality" (226). Taking well-known Lacanian formulae as interpretative keys, Garber then translates *The Roaring Girl*'s elements into their unconscious counterparts: "Moll is the phallus" (227); "In *The Roaring Girl* the lack is multiply overdetermined" (227); "Sir Alexander, who could be said to represent the stereotypical male gaze throughout the play . . ." (228). But is a succession of sexual and transvestite allusions and actions, converted into a Lacanian problematic, a logic? Have we entered an unconscious realm whenever we touch upon implicit references to sexuality? Have we grasped a totality of "inner dynamics"?

Not yet. Garber may rightly say the play dramatizes "the commutability of class and gender as categories capable of anxious social disruption" (222), but that does not mean there is a systematic logic of transvestism at work enacting that commutability. (How the adjective "anxious" can modify "social disruption" is unclear. People are anxious, disruptions are not.) She may have isolated some inner dynamic in the play's treatment of marriage and in the characters' anxieties about masculinity, but her argument still does not declare exactly what is the logic of the transvestite. She refers to "the play's logic" at the end of a paragraph on the two female characters' opposing attitudes toward marriage (Moll dismisses it, Mary desires it), but the paragraph offers no concrete referent for the term. It makes the point that the two ostensibly opposed characters, in fact, harbor both contrary attitudes and that each manifests openly but one, the inner division and its repressed side returning in the form of cross-dressing. This is an interesting thesis. But it is not a logic.

Now, for the second example.

When Fredric Jameson broaches the "cultural logic of late capitalism," he uses interpretative strategies that are neither empirical nor comprehensive. In his opening chapter, Jameson proposes to outline the constitutive attributes of the postmodern in order to develop a historical concept of postmodernism. Jameson interprets postmodernism not as a style, but as a realization of the dominant historical fact of our time: the rise of multinational capitalism. Postmodern art, literature, architecture, music, and so on are concrete sites wherein the forces, tendencies, and politics—in a word, the "logic"—of late capitalism are deployed. By analyzing characteristic postmodern features in light both of ideas of consumption, exchange, and reproduction and of knowledge of economic and social institutions, Jameson intends to divine the determining logic at work in present-day cultural and social life. There is no problem in the circularity of this method. Choosing certain objects as postmodern and reading them in order to build up a concept of postmodernism is an entirely legitimate procedure. However, if the resulting concept is going to be accurate and useful, if it is to apply smoothly to all the cultural products that Jameson wants it to, then the sample from which he infers the concept must be large and diverse. If the concept purports to have a descriptive benefit, if it claims to describe a social setting as complex and multifarious and disorienting as postmodern culture, then the sources of the concept must be versatile and many.

How does this requirement stand in Jameson's analysis? Aside from casual references to various art works and artists, here is the material he chooses to generalize from: two pages on Vincent Van Gogh's *A Pair of Boots*, two pages on Andy Warhol's *Diamond Dust Shoes*, three pages on Edvard Munch's *The Scream*, a paragraph on the Wells Fargo Court building in Los Angeles, a page of references to "nostalgia films" (*American Graffiti* and *Chinatown*, among others), four pages on E. L. Doctorow's *Ragtime*, a page on Bob Perelman's poem "China," four pages on John Portman's Westin Bonaventure Hotel, and finally a page on Michael Herr's *Dispatches*. Interspersed in Jameson's commentary are brief citations of Heidegger, Lacan, Guy Debord, Diego Rivera, Ernest Mandel, William Gibson, and numerous other artists and thinkers. He also includes several methodological observations on the difficulty of isolating and assessing a concept as shifty in its usages and uncanny in its apparitions as is "postmodernism."

After the forty-odd pages of mini-exegeses, Jameson writes, "The conception of postmodernism outlined here is a historical rather than a merely stylistic one" (45), a statement implying the conceptualization is complete. Then, he notes "the radical distinction between a view for which the postmodern is one (optional) style among many others available and a view which seeks to grasp it as the cultural dominant of the logic of late capitalism" (45–46), the latter being Jameson's own view. But have Jameson's discussions produced a sufficiently clear and distinct conception of postmodernism? Have they tied the postmodern to the "logic of capitalism"? Has the *logic* of capitalism been at all determined? Jameson's commentaries are clever and stimulating, but are they adequate evidence of the "logic of late capitalism"? Does a four-page analysis of the Bonaventure Hotel constitute proof of a postmodern condition? Does a hasty pastiche of two paintings of shoes, two buildings in L.A., a Language poem, a historical novel, a Vietnam report, Lacan's concept of the Imaginary, and Althusser's concept of Ideology—does this genuinely represent the postmodern? If one wishes to draw conclusions about contemporary culture at large, can a poem here, a painting there, a hotel here, and a theory there meet the basic standards of valid induction?

The dearth of subject matter in Jameson's outline is not the only argumentative flaw undermining the credibility of his generalizations. The analyses themselves, apart from some casual objective description, are highly conjectural. For example, in observing the interior of the Bonaventure, he surmises, "it seems to me that the escalators and elevators here henceforth replace movement but also, and above all, designate themselves as new reflexive signs and emblems of movement proper" (42). Jameson's inference here is problematic because his overall intent is an empirical one: to diagnose a historical situation. But his diagnosis rests upon speculative criticisms, upon dubious inferences (elevators as "emblems of movement proper") that provide little in the way of empirical support. Jameson offers readings, not demonstrations, imaginative interpretations that are neither falsifiable nor verifiable. Given Jameson's purpose, one would expect more of: 1) economic data— who owns the Bonaventure? how much did it cost to build? who financed it? how successful is the enterprise?; 2) historical data— who commissioned the architect? did the owners approve the plans? how often has the style been copied? how has it affected the downtown area?; 3) social data—who stays in the hotel? who works there? what does the community think of the building? what kinds of prestige does it bear? (In "Urban Renaissance and the Spirit of Postmodernism," Mike Davis poses just these questions.) If Jameson desires to read sociohistorical forces such as late capitalism through cultural products like the Bonaventure, surely the answers to these questions can place him on much firmer ground than do the speculative conclusions he draws.

But instead of addressing empirical facts, or at least adding them to his interpretations, Jameson reads the form and content of postmodern instances and surmises a representative postmodern-ness in them. So, after isolating the "postmodern hyperspace" of the Bonaventure, in whose dizzying maze of skylights, balconies, escalators, lounges, and corridors bewildered persons try to get their bearings, Jameson can make his "principal point":

> It may now be suggested that this alarming disjunction between the body and its built environment . . . can itself stand as the symbol and analogon of that even sharper dilemma which is the incapacity of our minds, at least at present, to map the great global multinational and decentered communicational network in which we find ourselves caught as individual subjects. (44)

This is the pivotal historical import of the Bonaventure, the essence of its postmodernity: visitors' incapacity to get their bearings within the hotel's space parallels individual subjects' incapacity to cognize the global, decentered world capitalism and technology have created. However, if this postulated resemblance is the upshot of Jameson's analysis, why does he offer it only as a "suggestion," one tentatively put forward ("may," "can")? If Jameson seeks to establish a determinate relation between postmodernism and the cultural logic of late capitalism, why does the Bonaventure enjoy only the uncertain status of symbol or "analogon"? For a symbolic or analogous relation does not at all imply a causal or logical connection. Though symbolic or analogous, the correspondence between the Bonaventure experience and the postmodern experience per se may be entirely factitious. The two experiences may be in some way isomorphic, but isomorphism demonstrates nothing but formal similarity. If this is the only relation Jameson poses between them, then the other claims made about the informing cultural logic of the Bonaventure space and that space's relation to late capitalism, as well as the nature of the logic of late capitalism itself, remain unsubstantiated.

This is not to criticize Jameson's entire argument, but only one aspect of it—its faulty derivation of a general logic. And the fault does not invalidate Jameson's contention on this account, but only shows its incompleteness. Furthermore, this incompleteness indicates why Jameson and others searching out a historical process and structure use the word "logic" instead of "workings," "economics," "conceptual structure," or "ideological structure." If critics invoking a "logic of" formulation chose instead a "workings of," "economics of," or "politics of" formulation, the words' materialist associations would compel them to support their interpretations with statistics, facts, reports, and testimony. Information would have to take the place of speculation. Empirical research would constitute the whole of the matter, for a "workings of" proposition demands no more than an empirical description. Other than those relatively simple principles basic to an empirical approach to things, no theoretical axioms or speculative inferences are needed for a satisfactory explanation of what the "workings of x" is. Inquirers would relinquish their theorist identities and instead become ordinary researchers gathering data, compiling figures, interviewing people. (Needless to say, the requisite documentation and field work take a lot more time and effort than does speculative interpretation.) The inquiry would be not an ideological diagnosis of a global postmodern condition, but a historical description of some concrete phenomenon. One might draw global conclusions from those descriptions, but only after filling the descriptions out with a sufficient amount of empirical information.

"Logic" provides a methodological shortcut. By virtue of its formal connotations, the term ostensibly allows critics to bypass empirical demonstration, fact gathering, classification of particulars, and so on. In citing a historical logic instead of historical workings, critics need only isolate a few abstract laws and relations and then plug in a few examples. And if someone were to judge that inquiry as too rarefied, the critics can respond that these abstractions do in fact derive from and apply to historical process, to real people, things, and events. In other words, the "logic of" convention lets critics have it both ways, broach historical realities without the labor of historiographical documentation. Critics outlining the "logic of x" may appear to engage with historical reality without getting bogged down in particulars, without letting the plurality of persons, facts, events, and causes cloud critics' apprehension of the logic informing these objects. That way, "logic of" analysis may be historical but not positivistic, formal but not transcendent. To cite Jameson again, " 'Analysis' I take to be that peculiar and rigorous conjuncture of formal and historical analysis that constitutes the specific task of literary and cultural study" (298). Historians may carry out the empirical task of data collection, logicians the academic task of proposition analysis. Literary and cultural critics combine the two projects into an interpretative strategy yielding a new disciplinary hybrid: the logic itself, that is, the part-historical and part-formal, half-structural and half-processual, part-ideal and part-factual dynamic at work in cultural phenomena. This new object of formal-historical study, a somewhat shadowy composite entity, allows critics to skirt the methodological standards of empirical research, be it the compilation of data or the analysis of causal relations. The "rigorous conjuncture of formal and historical analysis" validates half-hearted gestures in each direction, a weak sample of historical material and a partial examination of operative concepts.

The result is that "historical workings" critics derive a part-causal, part-ideological logic from meager and ambiguous historical materials, but the "logic of" reference saves them from historiographical attack. First, the application of "logic" to historical processes shields criticism from the charge of being a sterile, abstract formalism. Second, its formalist vestiges save critics from having to satisfy empirical standards of description and classification of historical data. Claiming these processes amount to a logic supposedly frees critics from performing exhaustive inquiry, for once they have isolated the phenomenon's organizing features, a few instances of it will suffice. A logic will reveal the phenomenon's necessity and completeness. Why bother with the dirty work of classifying a bunch of cultural particulars if we have already grasped their basic informing principles?

As for critics detailing a structure of textual workings, "logic" satisfies a similar methodological hastiness. It allows the critic to convert the text into a differential system of overdetermined epiphenomena. All the elements of the text—its actions, characters, metaphors, and so on—are but manifestations of a deeper regulatory organization. Having determined this master mechanism, the critic may move on to other things. Why bother to detail all those particulars once we have unveiled their informing principle?

The "logic of" usage makes interpretation and scholarship easier and quicker, while not making it appear superficial and haphazard. It shortens research time and lightens evidentiary demands. Because of logic's association with necessity and exactitude, the usage seems rigorous and expert. Logic critics are textual scientists.

political criticism The term "political criticism" denotes any kind of criticism that both puts writings in political contexts and is aware of its own political contexts. That is about as specific as the label gets. Often defined more in opposition to apolitical discourse than in favor of any particular political position, political criticism eschews all formalist purity and critical disinterestedness. Or rather, when it does broach such aesthetic ideas and practices, it does so through the politics of them. And this politicization of criticism does not involve an application of political attitudes to criticism, but the recognition that criticism has been political all along. For, critics argue, the apolitical presentations of previous schools of criticism merely mark critics' flight from political realities and disguise criticism's support for the status quo. To counteract that political bad faith, political criticism faces up to the inevitable politics that inform every critical act and judges those acts accordingly. Political criticism unveils the politics of this or that piece of literature and this or that critical practice and evaluates them on the basis of their political desirability.

Of course, the frank emphasis on political content as the criterion of value raises the now tiresome charge of political correctness. Such accusations are tiresome because they fail to appreciate the methodological handiness of political criticism and instead focus on its partisan aspects. What distinguishes today's political criticism from earlier versions of the discipline is the broad methodological shift it brings about. Specifically, what political criticism does is center criticism on political content and render formal, disciplinary, methodological considerations secondary. That is, with the rise of political content as the standard by which art, literature, and criticism are evaluated, other standards of evaluation decline in importance. These latter methodological standards include obedience to disciplinary conventions, depth and breadth of research, validity of argumentation, lucidity of style, and sophistication of ideas. Based upon training, logic, erudition, and eloquence, not on a particular political belief, these criteria are properly overlooked or minimized when a political critic-teacher conducts a tenure review of an assistant professor, writes a reader's report on a manuscript, concocts a course syllabus, or grades a paper. The professor determines the material's political assumptions and implications and evaluates it according to how closely it corresponds with a sanctioned political attitude. No matter how concisely reasoned, scrupulously documented, and intelligently expressed the material is, if it does not yield a particular political stance, it fails to qualify as worthwhile critical material. Perhaps it receives a qualified acknowledgment of intellectual or formal virtue from the political examiner, but its scholarly merits are quickly subordinated to its political shortcomings. On the other hand, if the material does have its political heart in the right place, any scholarly flaws it has are palliated by submitting them in to the larger question of the material's political probity. This is not because a political attitude argues that the intellectual or formal drawbacks are not drawbacks or that the formal or intellectual virtues are not virtues. A political understanding does not seriously address the work's formal or intellectual qualities as decisive. Evaluation rests upon a correspondence of a work's political particulars with a political standard, and other particulars do not substantially affect the correspondence. (The best gloss on the institutional nature of political evaluation in literary criticism is David Bromwich's *Politics by Other Means: Higher Education and Group Thinking.*)

Here is the methodological breakthrough of political criticism and teaching: not that it is political, but that its political priorities shortchange intellectual criteria. The term "political" announces a methodological displacement of method itself. Political criticism will not censure superficial research, shoddy argumentation, faulty citation, and inarticulate style in themselves, for it elevates a political agenda over other scholarly norms. Occasionally, one might hear political critics challenge many of those norms themselves, particularly formal ones, as conservative or reactionary, as institutional restraints hindering the progress of reform. But usually, political criticism prefers simply to ignore intellectual norms or to pay them minor lip service, not refute them. Indeed, the turn to politics obviates the need to refute at all. Politics merely displaces method, it does not falsify method. Political criticism strives to be transformative, not logical or methodological. It wants to change the world, not rehearse a discipline. Instead of asking of a new book, a graduate dissertation, or a sophomore paper "Does it substantiate its thesis?" professors of a political bent wonder "What political outlook does this imply?" Instead of judging a work of scholarship by its modes of verification, they judge it mainly by the political nature of the content being verified. On this political evaluation, which is entirely consistent with political premises, scholars and students heed first the overriding political aims, and make logical protocols and other formal requirements subsidiary to them.

This is not to say that political criticism is wrong, that teachers and scholars pushing for political interpretations of literature and language make false assertions. Indeed, because political criticism has canceled modes of verification, nonpolitical critics have no tools with which to counter political interpretations except political ones. This is one of political criticism's argumentative strengths. It absorbs all other types of criticism, makes them answer to its own principles and values. The term "political" has a capacity to color anything, to add a political slant to any activity or language, however apparently objective, logical, or scientific. So, political criticism cannot be falsified, for any attempted falsification can itself be understood politically. All anti-political critics can do (if they wish to converse with political critics) is argue over whether political critics' historical contentions and moral judgments are politically correct. The only kind of materials up for contention in political inquiry are political facts and political conclusions.

For example, a political analysis of American literary canon formation in the 1940s and '50s will flesh out various social and political biases that structured the canonical product. (The first volumes in Donald Pease's New Americanist Series are strong examples of this kind of project.) When it turns to the works canonized and not canonized at that time, the political analysis will reveal in them the qualities that reflect or contradict those biases. The works will respond, so to speak, to the political distinctions and concerns applied to them. That is how they will appear. A political survey of an American literary tradition, of its classics and non-classics as such, will interpret the materials within a political perspective and no further. A critic who wanted to do something more, say, to include within the general political discussion an analysis of a particular work's form and then relate that form to political issues, would (at least momentarily) have to change terms and methods of interpretation in order to satisfy formalist demands. He or she could not describe the work as a formal structure and simultaneously maintain a political commentary upon it. The critic may submit the formal analysis to political significance, but the formal analysis, in so far as it is a formal analysis, does not raise political concerns.

A related example: if a critic embarks upon a historicopolitical project of overcoming repressive canonical principles and recovering forgotten texts, then the critic will begin by demonstrating how these materials did not meet the canon requirements. As a political activity, the project will treat this incompatibility as a political difference and the recuperated text will have significance in so far as it diverges from the political attitudes that repressed it. The critic will select those elements in the text that led to its dismissal, those characters, actions, and styles that offended the canonizers' political sensibility. Because that politics now appears insupportable, the work gains political value and returns to critical attention. In order for the work to have another kind of value—aesthetic, historical, emotional, and so on—another kind of inquiry with its own less than wholly politicized concepts and methods must begin. The critic may proceed to give that other value a political significance, but the determination of the other value itself as an other value must be enacted on other than political grounds. The aesthetic or other value may be said to occupy a political space, an institutional milieu, but that value still will have within that space its own non-political terms and rules of inquiry.

Critics who believe in the priority of method to content would say that political criticism's refusal to deal with texts apolitically indicates not the absolute truth of political criticism, but its partiality. The fact that readers must alter their interpretative machinery when discussing texts aesthetically, for instance, reveals not the spuriousness of aesthetic readings, but their distinctiveness. This does not mean that political criticism fails, but only that it carries out a political criticism and nothing else. The proof that literary criticism always has implicit political designs does not prove that literary criticism equals political criticism. A political study of literary criticism yields a politics of literary criticism, an ideology of the aesthetic, not an annulment of literary criticism. Once one decides to do strictly literary criticism, though the decision itself may be political, the resulting methods and contents of any particular literary analysis must cohere with the concepts and strategies of literary analysis as a whole, not with political considerations. Once one adopts an aesthetic framework and goal, one proceeds in accordance with aesthetic definitions and distinctions.

A methodologist's point would be that a political analysis of x emerges from a methodological framework of political concepts and political arguments. Likewise, an aesthetic analysis of x emerges from an aesthetic methodological framework. Add a concept like politics to the aesthetic framework and you change all the constituents of it, as well as the framework itself. Hence, a concept of politics can apply to an aesthetic methodology only from the outside, for an aesthetic methodology relies precisely on the exclusion of political concerns for its own internal coherence. One may make political judgments of this or that aesthetic theory and practice as a whole, but one cannot accept the concepts and methods of an aesthetic theory and perform a political analysis with them. To introduce politics into aesthetics is to de-aestheticize it, to explode it. Of course, one can take aesthetics and its institutional practice as having clear political implications and effects in this or that context, but the conceptual structure and evaluative standards of aesthetics do not include political concepts and standards within their make-up. What we do with an aesthetic framework in any particular situation is clearly a non-aesthetic question, but because there is no necessary relation between an aesthetic and the ways it gets used politically, we need not include political concepts in our inventory of aesthetic structures. The only way to justify making an internal politicization of aesthetics and disrupting the aesthetic conceptual field would be to say that the field is false and misrepresentative if it lacks a political concept.

This latter judgment is, in fact, where the term "political" gets its force. It seems to have a universal applicability, to predicate every institutional act scholars and teachers commit. Whereas aesthetic, psychological, linguistic, and other methods of reading and evaluation operate on their own distinct rules, politics pertains to any rule-governed behavior. Methods may be distinct from one another on conceptual and practical grounds, but they all have their politics. Hence, because "political" applies to all methods, political criticism subsumes all other criticisms. Method-minded critics who limit political criticism to a political sphere evade the truth that politics is the root substance of institutional reality. Apolitical criticism is simply hidden political criticism. Apolitical criticism may transmit an emotional, aesthetic, or psychological understanding of discourse, but those foci only seem apolitical by virtue of their blindness to their own political contexts.

The utterance of "political" serves to underscore the ultimately political character of all conduct. Political critics announce the political meaning of inquiry and, thereby, shift debate onto political grounds. All inquiry follows a "politics of" scheme. No longer need critics meet formalists and psychologists on formal and psychological footings. All footings are political, and so the most abstract propositions, rules, and canons of reasoning solicit a political analysis. Having achieved the insight that all kinds of institutional behavior are the product and instrument of social forces and political interests, critics may turn to a discovery of the behavior's tools for organizing the world into fields of analysis, for defining institutional settings and patrolling disciplinary borders, for supplying members with principles of exclusion, for legitimizing statements that meet the institution's reproductive needs. "Political" is a broadside term eliminating methodological distinctions, saving critics from having to argue with nonpolitical critics and teachers on nonpolitical grounds.

problematize   We all know what "problematize" means: to make something taken for granted, a putative given, a cozily familiar object, or an unconscious assumption problematic. To problematize *x* is to take an entity that has conventional status (for whatever reasons, be they psychological, institutional, or political) and uncover problems that lurk in its genesis or its effects. The routine nature of the entity is held up to criticism and the entity itself comes to be seen with an acute skepticism by critics. If a concept or category has settled into a customary way of thinking or judging, if a text has been interpreted into seeming transparency, if an event has been transformed into a set of discrete known and rational facts, then we have been lured into a false sense of epistemological security. We have traded a wary acknowledgment of the complexity of all things and the interestedness of our researches for a reassuring certitude that all things may be comprehended and that our comprehension is not based on partisan needs. We save ourselves from such false consciousness, from the natural attitude, from theoretical blindness, and from empirical naïvetés by problematizing the concepts and objects we have lived unreflectively. In analyzing the conceptual components and relations of *x*, in exploring the conditions of *x*'s assumption to given-ness, in noting the contingencies of its use, in short, in asking a series of theoretical and pragmatic questions about *x*, we dissolve its self-evidence. *X* becomes problematic. From then on, we must treat *x* critically, qualify our affirmation of it, attend to the problems embedded within it.

   This is not to say that *x* should be removed from critical discourse, but only that *x* has a complex status and that critics should handle *x* with care, fully aware of *x*'s problematic implications. This newfound self-consciousness purportedly marks an advance in criticism, one of criticism's purposes being to save inquiry from thoughtless assertions and unfounded positions, or rather, from assertions and positions founded upon spurious closures, concealed decisions, institutional pressures, narrow self-interest. A problematized x will not lead critics who use it into an unwitting use of the problems of x. A deproblematized x (that is, a supposedly deproblematized x) is an epistemological seduction, an ostensibly workable constituent of thought (a concept, percept, principle, formula, etc.) whose suppressed problematics will ultimately resurface as systematic but unexpected inconsistencies. For in many cases, the de-problematizing gesture actually constitutes not a genuine resolution of things, but a repression of complications, an overlooking of difficulties. Often, unproblematic ideas and attitudes endure merely because of persons' mental complacency or because of political expediency. For example, the idea of a literary "classic" was unproblematic to Matthew Arnold, problematizing critics would say, because it provided certain private satisfactions and ideological benefits. (Arnold would in part agree.) If we problematize "classic," we make those private and public implications explicit, keep them from sinking into effects that we merely live through.

The act of problematizing has obvious rhetorical uses. It sounds rigorous and powerful as a weapon in the fight against lax and dishonest inquiry. Also, for trained critics, problematizing x is one of the easiest interpretative gestures to make. In the most basic instance, all one has to do is add quotation marks to x, to say "*Walden* is a 'classic' " instead of "*Walden* is a classic." The scarequotes cause a hesitation over the term and imply a set of other problematizing questions: what is a "classic"? what does it presuppose? in what contexts is it used? what does it do? what educational and political purposes does it serve? Instead of being a familiar predicate in scholarship, one readers casually assimilate without much notice, "classic" now stands out from the flow of discourse. The questions hover around its use and, until they are resolved, the use of "classic" is impaired.

Usually, such questions yield ready answers, but their readiness does not cut into the apparent savviness of the critics asking them. This is another advantage of the term "problematize": it is a simple procedure, but it sounds like an incisive investigative pursuit. The line of response to the "problematizing" of "classic" might run: a "classic" is an institutional construct developed by an educated class, an idea presupposing mutually supportive concepts of art, genius, and nationality, used strategically in places where the educated class reproduces itself. A "classic" is not (as the old line would have it) an extra-historical object originating in some otherworldly inspiration that persons should come to appreciate or be culturally damned. Given this debunking of the "classic," this exposure of "classic"'s actual genesis and function, the term now is problematic, politically loaded, methodologically suspect, under erasure.

This complication of accepted ideas and values certifies the critic's heightened awareness. As a problematizer, the critic is sensitive to institutional contexts and dubious of interpretative habits. What others handle with thoughtless facility, the problematizer queries with wary deliberation. He is a conceptual devil's advocate, an anti-positivist gadfly who keeps inquiry honest, preventing other inquirers from relying uncritically upon problematic norms and methods.

But, one might ask, what else does the problematizer do? What becomes of his or her particular problematizations? The term "classic" has been problematized, but what then? This elementary gesture only marks the first step in the reconstruction of inquiry. To problematize "classic," to show that "classic" has a complex political value or that it presumes some equivocal concepts, rightly initiates not a removal of the term, but a re-examination of it. Though the term's problematics indicate a political bias or a conceptual difficulty, these implications are matter for discussion, evaluation, revision. To prove that "classic" is a political convention or a conceptual invention makes no difference unless we decide then to alter the construct (since in practice, constructions can be just as binding as universals). Just because x can be called into question does not mean that x no longer has any methodological value. Its very questionability does not make it unsound. We may problematize x, but what we do with x after that depends upon how we assess the new awareness of x's problems, and that latter investigation is not a mode of problematizing. We problematize x in order to improve upon it, to exercise quality control of it, not to level charges against it. We raise questions about x to answer them.

But the answers are rarely forthcoming. For instance, in "The Postmodern Problematizing of History," Linda Hutcheon argues that postmodernism poses difficulties for historians that the old historiographical methods cannot overcome. Postmodernism "problematizes the entire notion of historical knowledge" (367), this by showing that "both history and fiction are discourses, that both constitute systems of signification by which we make sense of the past" (367). History is not just the innocent recall of what happened, but rather a "discourse" of the past with its own codes and conventions. This is a problematizing recognition because it implies that "the meaning and shape are not *in the events*, but *in the systems* which make those events into historical facts" (367). So, positivist and empiricist assumptions about history no longer hold (373) and a new textual and discursive understanding of even the most basic historical facts must commence.

This is by now a humdrum argument in scholarship and it takes little critical intelligence to assert that the concepts and language of history shape the objects of historical inquiry. (Also, this problem originates not in postmodernism, but in nineteenth-century hermeneutics.) A curious thing about Hutcheon's essay, then: why does it supply nothing to clear this problem up? why does it give no counsel as to how to conduct historical interpretation in a postmodern world? Hutcheon outlines the problematic, contests history, and stops. She affirms only the continuous problematizing of postmodern practice: "the unresolved tensions of postmodern aesthetic practice remain paradoxes or contradictions" (379). Such tensions as those between historical fact and historiographic method, between an event and the signifying system one uses to describe the event, do not go away. History remains problematized. But why not make adjustments in history that will accommodate postmodern realities? Why not attempt a solution to the problem?

In general, why concentrate so much on problematization? First, because if critics move beyond the problematization toward some resolution, they lose their status as problematizers, as shrewd questioners of sedimented values and customary practices. The prestige they garner as inquiry watchdogs dissipates as soon as they begin to endorse some element of inquiry. Indeed, as soon as they cease problematizing things, critics themselves become liable to problematization. The concepts and attitudes they accept become targets for other problematizers and the former problematizers begin to look just as naive and complicitous as the critics they previously problematized. In maintaining the problematizing perspective, critics enjoy the comforts of negativity, for in problematizing all things they need affirm nothing.

the question of   This phrase often pops up in criticism as an announcement of theme. Critics title their books and essays with headings like *Daemonic Figures: Shakespeare and the Question of Conscience*, "History, Poststructuralism, and the Question of Narrative," *Ortega y Gassett and the Question of Modernity*, "Molly's Flow: The Writing of 'Penelope' and the Question of Women's Language," and "Lacan and the Question of Writing." The phrase serves to set off a topic, to take a concept, an entity, or an event and make it into a question, a site of interrogation. In such usages, conscience, modernity, women's language, writing, and the like become not simply objects of straightforward curiosities like "when does modernity begin?" or "how does the syntax of women's language work?" or "is writing more expressive than speech?" or "what kind of narratives does poststructuralism yield?" Instead of posing such regular empirical or semantic questions about some thing, the phrase "the question of *x*" puts *x* itself in question, holistically. The very existence, value, and purpose of *x* come under scrutiny, are bracketed for philosophical investigation. Now a focus of hermeneutical suspicion, *x* is lifted out of the routine configurations of discourse and practice and set into the speculative light. What then follows is no ordinary discussion of *x*, no normal accounting of its invention, its attributes, its conceptual makeup and pragmatic uses. A "question of" criticism produces a profound inquisition into the wellsprings of *x*'s being.

The attention to the roots of *x*'s meaning and being indicates the origin of the "question of" usage: Heidegger's *Being and Time*. There, particularly in the Introduction, Heidegger makes the conversion from an object of study to a question into a decisive hermeneutical habit. Although Heidegger has phenomenological precursors who similarly pose the fundamental question of this or that concept or entity, for literary and cultural critics Heidegger's masterwork stands, however dimly, as the source of the interpretative gesture signalled by the "question of" formula. For, from the opening pages of *Being and Time*, Heidegger gears his entire argument toward a single question, a crucial but forgotten call to genuine thinkers: the question of Being. Indeed, he claims, any interpretation of Being must begin not with a statement of what Being is, but rather an acknowledgment of "*The Necessity of Explicitly Restating the Question of Being*" (22). An inquiry into Being must first examine the angle of inquiry, the question that prompts and, in a way, predetermines the answer that will conclude the inquiry. In not proceeding headlong into a description of what is, in pausing over the seemingly self-evident idea of is-ness, in interrogating one conceptual tool of ontological inquiry, Heidegger proceeds on surer philosophical ground, more aware of the cognitive prejudices that might obscure the unconcealment of Being. And, one might add, Heidegger does not answer the question "What is Being?" Instead, for the next five hundred pages, Heidegger deliberates with a ponderous intensity the question of Being and the questioner of Being (*Dasein*).

In Heidegger's hands, this is a masterful procedure. Its hermeneutical power is infectious. Heidegger sets the authentic thinker apart, divides inquirers up into two camps: the naive, cognitively complacent, positivistic answerers and the wisely hesitant, cognitively dissatisfied, speculatively acute questioners. While the former use Being thoughtlessly, as a cognitive habit, Heidegger poses anew the question of Being and thereby prevents himself from using or thinking Being in a casual, traditional manner. The question marks a capaciousness of mind and distinguishes the questioner as a superior observer of Western thought. Once Heidegger transforms Being from a presupposed notion into an analyzable concept, he empowers his inquiry, assumes control over what was heretofore passively assumed: "Of course 'Being' has been presupposed in all ontology up till now, but not as a *concept* at one's disposal—not as the sort of thing we are seeking" (27). When one adopts the "question of" investigative posture, even Being itself lies at one's disposition. The inherited ways of cognizing the world, always a function of cognitive laziness and group coercion, no longer master the inquisitive mind (see *Being and Time*, 43). Fundamental concepts like Being are no longer realities persons undergo. They are cognitive tools persons wield in a limited way and are partly responsible for.

No wonder the "question of" usage appeals to critics. The speculative sophistication and dignity it bears flatter critics who worry over their philosophical prowess. The hermeneutical bracketing it entails reflects critics' independent discernment, their resistance to customary ways of seeing. The conceptual empowerment it produces palliates critics' insecurity about the potency of their labors and grants them greater responsibility for their intellectual actions (so that they avoid bad faith). The "question of" formulation means intellectual power and moral scrupulousness.

However, notwithstanding its philosophical seductions, the usage has a singular disadvantage. Its utterance forces critics to carry out a sustained, concentrated deliberation over the question itself, to posit nothing that might smack of an overhasty, too familiar resolution of the question at issue. More simply, if a critic proposes to explore the question of conscience, modernity, writing, narrative, and so on, the critic cannot proceed to answer the question. He or she must for a time eschew empirical descriptions and dictionary definitions of the thing in question, to remain at a level of abstraction, to examine the question from a variety of speculative viewpoints. Such painstaking conceptual analyses require that critics direct their interpretations against the grain of conventional critical habits, that they exercise patience in their progress from one point to the next (a difficult task given today's accelerating publication pressures), and that they understand all the presuppositions, concept-formations, and sedimented attitudes surrounding and informing the entity in question.

These strict intellectual obligations might seem to mitigate the "question of" usage's attractiveness, especially for shorter scholarly essays. But that is not the case, for criticism has developed a way to make the "question of" citation and enjoy its dignities *and* skip the methodological follow-up burdens of it: to ignore them. This is the pattern of "question of" usage in criticism today. Critics pose the question of *x* (again, not just *a* question, but *the* question) and then leave it hanging. They insert the question of modernity, writing, and so on into titles, introductory remarks, thesis statements, and topical descriptions, but rarely do they articulate and clarify the question in the arguments and evidence that follow. It is almost as if critics believe that merely stating "the question of *x*" adequately identifies a field of inquiry.

For example, in "The Question of Agency: Michel de Certeau and the History of Consumerism," Mark Poster discusses de Certeau's work and its tenuous relations with Marxism and with cultural studies. The analysis is clear and informative and one leaves the essay with a desire to read de Certeau's work carefully and appreciate its value to current institutions of criticism. But, as a treatment of the question of agency, the essay is a disappointment. It never says exactly what the question of agency is. It alludes briefly to the "poststructuralist critique of the subject as author" (100), an issue that certainly bears upon agency, but Poster does not pursue the issue at all. He later refers to the "idea of a free social agent" and notes the suspect belief in the "liberal-Marxist agent who is already free, centered, and rational" (101). Readers could infer a host of questions of agency from these sentences—does a free social agent exist? is rationality or centered-ness necessary to agency?—but Poster does not indicate what is *the* question embedded in them. Apparently, the question is so obvious that no further specifications are needed. Finally, in the last paragraph, Poster mentions "the problem of agency or practice" (106), but he does not verbalize those problems or differentiate them. ("Agency" and "practice" are not synonymous, nor for that matter are "problem" and "question.") So, what is the problem? What is the question? Why is the phrase "the question of agency" in the title of this essay?

Poster's article fails to uphold the promise of its title (though it succeeds in other ways), but at least it gestures distantly toward the question at hand. In many other instances, critics do not even touch upon the issue advertised at the beginning of the piece. Lawrence Buell's "Melville and the Question of American Decolonization" does not assert a single definite thing about the question of American decolonization (whatever that question may be). Nor does Arkady Plotnisky's "The Medusa's Ears: The Question of Nietzsche, the Question of Gender, and Transformations of Theory" anywhere provide even a modest sample of the question of Nietzsche (again, whatever that may be). In "Ambiguity and Alienation in *The Second Sex*," Toril Moi introduces a passage from Simone de Beauvoir with the sentence, "Starting where *The Ethics of Ambiguity* ends, *The Second Sex* launches its inquiry into women's condition by focusing on the question of difference" (97–98). But the passage contains absolutely nothing resembling a question. Moi follows the quotation with the assertion, "Beauvoir here poses a radically new theory of sexual difference." Does this mean that "question" and "theory" are synonymous? That the theory answers the question? Joseph A. Boone's and Michael Cadden's Introduction to a volume entitled *Engendering Men: The Question of Male Feminist Criticism* insists that male feminist criticism "remains, and ought to remain, a question, rather than a definitive classification" (2). How a label can be a question and how a question and a classification can function as alternatives remain (but ought not to remain) unsaid. The next sentence merely continues the guarded urgency of the previous: "The 'question of male feminist criticism,' that is, must necessarily remain such so long as men live in a society in which most of our sex . . . have been, and continue to be, the beneficiaries of an asymmetrical sexual system that oppresses women." One might agree with the sentiment expressed here, but what is the referent for "question"? The editors never pin down the object, never specify the *question* of male feminist criticism. Boone and Cadden say the question must "necessarily remain such," but they do not provide the "such."

A final example: a collection of impressive essays of philosophical criticism entitled *Literature and the Question of Philosophy*, edited and introduced by Anthony Cascardi. Not one of the individual pieces in the volume uses the "question of" phrasing, so one would expect to find the question expressed in the Introduction. But there, all that appears is an assertion that "the interrelationship of literature and philosophy throughout their history has been problematized" (x). One assumes this problematical interrelation translates into a question about philosophy, or rather, the question of philosophy. But though the Introduction and each essay pore over the philosophy-literature agon, none of them isolate the concomitant question. The only place the notion appears is in the book's title.

These publications exemplify the vacuousness of the "question of" usage. Ideally, the slogan functions as a speculative opening, a broad demarcation of concepts and entities to be interpreted gingerly but resolutely. The "question of" citation lays out a field of inquiry and serves the investigation as its quick and easy first step. But without the accompanying intensive conceptual and semantic analysis of the terms of the question, the announcement is hollow and hackneyed. This is not to say that the "question of" usage has no value to criticism. Occasionally, critics pose the question of *x* in explicit terms and proceed to examine it with all due specificity and resolve. (Judith Butler's "Contingent Foundations: Feminism and the Question of 'Postmodernism' " and Claude Rawson's " 'Indians' and Irish: Montaigne, Swift, and the Cannibal Question" are cases where a question is clearly stated and addressed.) But such exceptions are far outnumbered by the citation-without-clarification habit. Why do critics invoke such a transparently weak titular cliche?

First, as noted above, the "question of" phrasing grants the critic a philosophical command and a moral circumspection. In posing the question of *x* instead of proceeding to use *x*, critics guard against philosophical naïveté and destructive behavior. The gesture puts critics into the attitude of contemplation, where wisdom lies not in speedy affirmations of facts and verities, but in calm examinations of our conceptual instruments. This elevation of questioning over positing has a methodological advantage as well, which is the second reason critics raise the question of *x* and then let it disappear like a wisp of smoke. If a critic raises the question and makes that alone the object of the argument, he can meander around the question with a series of tangential observations and do so with seeming justification. Because he is operating in an interrogative mood, he need not make any positive assertions (which, of course, require logical and/or empirical evidence). Indeed, to posit anything would be to breach the questioning genre. The critic must remain in a tentative posture, must take no position on the question except that of opposing those who do take a position on it. Here is the great seduction of the "question of" usage: it validates the non-taking of a stand, apologizes for the absence of evidence, and even vindicates the absence of an explicit formulation of the question itself.

radical "Radical" is a term of multifarious meaning in critical discourse, so here I will focus on one particular usage: "radical" as an epistemological concept. This usage occurs when "radical" predicates an act of mind, as in the phrases "a radical interpretation of," "a radical reconfiguration of," "a radical concept of." The act deserves the adjective "radical" because it marks an epistemological breakthrough, a profound departure from past ways of thinking. The rationale goes like this: putatively objective principles and things and the distinctions built upon them are epistemologically grounded; they are tied to a way of conceiving, a cognitive attitude, and have no absolute claim on thinking itself; an adherence to certain habits of inquiry and their objects equals an obedience to certain mental habits of inference; if those habits are broken, a radical transformation of things has taken place. "Radical" here signifies an epistemic revolution, a fundamental change in basic perceptions. Mind itself changes, not just its contents. One gestalt replaces another, and so the foundational postulates and preliminaries proper to the superseded ways of thinking become obsolete.

A crisis approach to inquiry is indicated by the use of the term "radical." When applied to a theoretical development like deconstruction or a technological development like the electronic text, it denotes not simply a shift of critical focus, an enlargement of a tradition, or a quickening of communication. Rather, it amounts to a radical break in the course of human thought. When such revolutionary epistemic shifts take place, our cognitive attitudes toward objects change and the objects, then, themselves change. The resulting radical discontinuity between the old cognitive attitude and the new prevents any methodological interaction between them. The differences between one mentality and another are deep and basic enough to render them incommensurable. The epistemes are entirely incongruous.

I will not enter into the epistemological and historical arguments on conceptual relativism. (Some basic texts are Thomas Kuhn's *The Structure of Scientific Revolutions*, Quine's *Word and Object*, and Davidson's "On the Very Idea of a Conceptual Scheme.") Instead, let us note a methodological advantage of the "radical" attribution: an end to discussion, an impossibility of debate. Since we have a radical disjunction of cognitive maps, a total incommensurability of conceptual frames, inquirers occupying different epistemes have no basis for agreement or disagreement. The standards of validity and even of intelligibility that each disputant operates on do not meet. If an "old" methodologician examines a "new" critical discourse and says, "There is a confusion here between empirical claims and the speculative evidence you use to support it," the "new" methodologician would not agree or disagree. He or she would merely say, perhaps, "Well, what you interpret as a confusion seems to me to be an inventive linkage of realms heretofore kept apart." If the "old" inquirer responds, "But they should be kept apart for reasons of coherence," the "new" inquirer could rejoin, "No, they have been kept apart only because your conceptual system would not admit their collocation." Construing the value of the empirical-speculative division contrariwise, the rivals have no basis for engagement, no fundamental accord as to the protocols of analysis. "Old" and "new" inquirers have no common starting point, for their cognitive predispositions are radically disparate, as are their basic apprehensions of the same phenomena. In addressing basic facts and blank objects, old and new inquirers actually see and describe and judge different things.

What this means is that inquirers inhabiting different epistemic attitudes cannot talk about the same things (there are no same things) nor can they talk about discrepancies between dissimilar things (because there are no same words). From one episteme to another, there is no common perception and there is no common language or metalanguage. (Even if such a metalanguage did exist, there would be no way of verifying that users were using it in the same way and meaning the same thing by it.) In other words, in pushing radical epistemological difference, conceptual relativists create a situation of non-communication. They deny any basis for comparing objects, words, and analytic strategies coming from divergent cognitive attitudes. In affirming that methodological criteria are proper to but one cognitive sphere, conceptual relativists contain them and shelter other conceptualizations from them. They forestall any accusations of methodological violation. In this outlook, we have not a hierarchy of right and wrong, true and false, valid and invalid, but instead a field of different and incomparable ways of thinking about things. If a positivist objects to a postmodernist's interpretation on the grounds that the interpretation does not follow standard verification procedures, the postmodernist does not reply by trying to show that the interpretation does follow standard verification procedures. Instead, the postmodernist responds with a blank non-recognition of positivist verification. To do otherwise, even to argue for or against the validity of verification, would be to imply that the positivist and postmodernist standpoints are not as radically different as they are so often trumpeted to be. If the differences become communicable, even if still unresolvable, then positivist and postmodernist share some epistemic material and the changes in forms of inquiry amount to an adjustment of terms and methods, not a cognitive revolution.

Clinging to the radical purport of cognitive difference, radical critics do not falsify, invalidate, or delegitimize one cognitive scheme or another. They simply allow for one to dismiss all the others. (Of course, dismissal is itself a form of recognition and signifies some shared conceptual understanding, but we will not quibble.) One scheme's semantic clarity and methodological commitment does not match another's, so they have nothing to discuss. Contemporary inquirers who have broken with the past see no point in debating the past, for they discern no import in it. The radical epistemic principle demands that all intellectual practices be related to minds and their language, world view, conceptual frame, and cognitive attitude. Since these mental and linguistic structures each constitute a totality, since they are untranslatable (since there is no criterion of translatability that is not part of one structure or the other, we have no way of corroborating the correct translation of pieces of one structure into the other), we end up with two persons who cannot speak to one another. There is no disputing mental taste. A conceptual framework is epistemologically organized and a mind is constituted within and confined by the framework. So one mind can look at another mind from another framework only as foreign, nonsensical, absolutely beside the point.

Of course, a pragmatic solution to the conversational breakdown of epistemic relativism emerges as soon as we realize that the putatively radical differences we find in various interpretive perspectives only make sense against a background of shared belief. For differences among inquirers and their attitudes to be intelligible, inquirers must possess a relatively large number of similar ideas and attitudes. If we have intelligible differences, then first of all we must have a common language within which those differences are intelligible and communicable, and that language itself signifies innumerable tacit agreements the thinkers have made. Even the assertion of radical difference implies some communication, for as soon as the radical thinker asserts the obsolescence of the older thinking, he or she admits to interpreting the latter and contradicts the assertion of utter incomparability. So, there is no epistemological reason why inquirers insist upon the radical character of their respective positions.

But there is an institutional reason: inquirers wish to free themselves from facing certain arguments. This is what the "radical" citation does: it discounts the relevance of certain forms of thinking. By asserting a radical difference between one interpretation, analysis, reasoning and another, a critic silences the refutation of one by the other. The term "radical" breaks down communication. It is an argumentative dead end constituted for a purpose. Anyone outside the radical way of thinking has no rejoinder.

rethink   This term signifies a thorough examination of fundamental assumptions and first principles. One rethinks an event, a
text, a fact, and so on by delving into the phenomenon's conceptual
make-up. On the anti-positivist supposition that any phenomenon
is shaped by concepts, values, interests, and perspectives, rethinking begins again from the beginning, strives to bring the phenomenon's most basic cognitive constituents to the surface so that it
may be interpreted anew. To rethink is not to re-observe or re-
describe or re-situate. It is to approach the phenomenon in such a
profound and original epistemological way that its very meaning
and the way we experience it change.

The justification for this assiduous, creative reconceptualization
of things is simple. Long a staple of phenomenological analysis,
rethinking keeps language from becoming too routine, concepts
from becoming too sedimented, and facts from becoming too factual. Rethinking works backward through the layers of opinion and
prejudice that gather around things and seemingly become natural
to them. This accretion of values and interests constitutes the experienced content of the thing, the "old" thinking that has con-
gealed into customary perceptions and fixed meanings. Breaking
through that crust of familiarized experience, rethinking conceives
things afresh. It struggles against the inertia of thought, the seductions of group thinking, and the psychic investments of habitual
cognition to deliver an original insight, a new angle of vision that
reveals both the deficiencies of the old thought and the possibility
of a new experience. The rethinking critic is the harbinger of conceptual innovation, the destroyer of routine interpretation. His cultural role is to guarantee the authenticity of experience, to oppose
the inevitable decline of insight into convention.

Such an office does honor to the critic, especially considering
how strenuous a successful rethinking is. A valid rethinking of x must
suspend the old concepts that formerly constituted the thought of
x—an arduous and highly self-critical procedure. As a whole, the
old thinking is too tacit, too ritualized, too familiar and satisfying
for thinkers merely to set it aside except by carrying out a laborious,
patient, and self-conscious analysis. If a conceptual scheme has become so common that it has sunk into unconsciousness, if a certain
mode of thinking has become so smooth-running that it fares implicitly with others' unreflective acceptance, it has done so for a
reason. The older thinking must serve certain ends expediently,

easefully. The reasons for its expeditiousness may be psychological or political, but in any case those who adopted the older thinking have personal and institutional investments in it. To override those satisfactions, to give up the prior thinking and establish a new meaning and value for the phenomenon requires intense concentration and commitment, a diligent non-conformity that resists the subtlest social and cultural coercions.

Even if one senses intellectual, moral, or political drawbacks in it, the prevailing thinking of x maintains a powerful claim on a mind's experience of x. The costs of abandoning a settled conceptualization are anxiety, cognitive disturbance, and alienation from old thinkers. Those thinkers who wish to continue their rethinking notwithstanding the personal and political risks it entails must relentlessly pursue their inquiries despite the recurrent temptation to resort to old habits of conceiving and the omnipresent pressure to comply with old institutions of interpretation. Even if they successfully resist such entrapments, rethinkers still face other problems, in particular, a cognitive dilemma: in every inference lies "an immense mass of cognition" (Charles Sanders Peirce's phrase), and to account for *that* mass requires another conceptual base that itself remains unaccounted for. There is no pure starting point for any inquiry. In even the most ruthless rethinking resides a functional, but unthought cognitive reservoir. So every rethinking must take off from some old basis. This problem does not discount rethinking, but it does force an acknowledgment of the complex preconditions of any particular rethinking interpretation.

These social and cognitive difficulties of rethinking testify to the mental independence and personal courage of the rethinker. To return to a phenomenon's conceptual wellsprings, a critic must undergo cognitive insecurity and institutional ostracism. To break with the prevailing conditions of interpretation, an inquirer risks both disciplinary condemnation and alienation from his or her own past tendencies of thought. To fulfill its transformative purpose and revise the foundations of the cognition of x, rethinking must proceed with caution, in full admission of its reliance upon other uninterrogated thoughts, its inclination toward cozy mental habits, and its tenuous progress toward new thoughts.

The intellectual daring of rethinking explains the popularity of the term in contemporary criticism. Despite the hazardousness of such epistemological journeys, the project of rethinking concepts and realities, texts and contexts, periods and periodicity, and so on has become one of criticism's most common practices. While the MLA Bibliography from 1963–80 lists only twelve titles containing the word "rethinking," for the years 1990–94 it shows one hundred forty-eight entries. In the last year, books have appeared with titles like "Rethinking Literary History," "Rethinking Metaphysics," "Rethinking Meter," "Rethinking Knowledge," "Rethinking the Political," "Rethinking the Subject." In the last few years, we have seen conferences on "Rethinking Women's Poetry, 1730–1930," "Re-thinking Translation," "Rethinking Family Values: Formations, Transformations, Resistances, Disillusions," "Perspectives on Witchcraft: Rethinking the Seventeenth-Century New England Experience," and "Rethinking the Eighteenth Century Garden." Given the awesome generality of such topics, it would seem that just about everything is undergoing the current generation's cognitive revisions. Everybody is doing it. The endeavor even has a collectivist slant, for many "rethinking" texts are collections of essays by different critics all engaged in rethinking an assigned object and many rethinking acts are carried out at academic gatherings like conferences and seminars. As a group activity, an institutional imperative, rethinking assembles critics into a community of interpreters, a collegial aggregate of inquisitive minds committed to the project of re-cognizing the world. Rethinking is now a sanctioned, routine critical practice, one whose parameters are apparently so familiar that critics can rethink virtually any scholarly topic at will if they find the right community.

To rethink x, one must have already thought through the terms and limits of the older thinking of x and determined their disadvantages. Then, one must decide what is the most advantageous cognitive base from which the new thinking of x should issue. Such crucial epistemological shifts take time and thoughtfulness. Given the complexities involved, one cannot rethink an x that springs from a long-standing tradition except through years of cogitation, historical research, and institutional implementation of the rethought x. For this reason, a book like Donald Preziosi's *Rethinking Art History: Meditations on a Coy Science* simply takes on too much too fast. How can a scholar rethink x in a hundred seventy-nine pages of text if x has the size of an entire discipline? No matter how much institutional experience and raw brilliance Preziosi possesses, his subject matter is too big to be rethought. There is too much conceptual and historical material to cover. (How much more rueful it is, then, to see "rethinking" essays that number only fifteen pages or to observe inexperienced inquirers like graduate students proffer to rethink *x* in their seminar papers and dissertations.)

All the more reason, then, to appropriate the term. When Drucilla Cornell begins "Rethinking the Beyond Within the Real (Response to Rasch)," she takes on massive metaphysical concepts like transcendence and reality and a daunting philosophical tradition (the essay refers to Kant, Wittgenstein, Derrida, Levinas, and Luhmann), all in eleven short pages. The rethinking concludes when Cornell conceives the beyond not as transcendence, but as utopian possibility, "a promise of a better world" (233). One might say that this is not a rethinking, but instead a simple, though broad revision of where one places the beyond, in a temporal realm, not in a metaphysical one. The term "rethinking" magnifies the revision into a profound meditation, an elemental departure from Western thought. That reflects well upon the critic. "Rethinking" grants the thinker a mastery over the material, a sophistication of attitude, an originality of approach. It consigns the past to antiquity and places the critic at the vanguard of thought. The difficulty of the endeavor solicits prudence from critics, but when the practice has become so common that it need not require justification, the elevation of critic into rethinker is a normal and necessary token of status.

sociology of literature   Formerly, this term designated an approach to literature through the window of a critical theory of society. Leading figures in this school were Georg Lukács, Leo Lowenthal, Theodor Adorno, and Raymond Williams. Today, however, the term names any kind of interdisciplinary activity that applies sociological concepts and contents to literary objects. As a combination of social science practices and humanities contents, sociology of literature appreciates aesthetic complexity, but attributes it to social conditions. Literature is preserved as a special category of culture, but its speciality resides in its squarely sociological meaning, not in its transcendence of social conditions. Sociology of literature is synthetic, conjoining the best empirical, information-producing elements of sociology with the textual subtleties and theoretical insights of literary criticism.

It is important to see "sociology of literature" as an interdisciplinary designation, not a pluralist one. It signifies a unification of approaches, not a diversity of them. Pluralism is not a mingling of methods, but a recognition that many methods have potentially equal value in the interpretation of an object. Because the object has so many cultural affiliations, historical inscriptions, and political uses, pluralism argues, no single method is adequate to it, so we need to tolerate a variety of interpretative attitudes toward it. And because those attitudes begin with different definitions of the object, because they mark from the start diverse methodological outlooks, they refuse to be united into a coherent super-method. Because they differ not simply in their representations of the object (which could be mutually corrigible), but in their definitions of it (which are axiomatic), the approaches are forever incompatible. If they were not so, if some super-method ever came about, pluralism would end.

This is why "sociology of literature" must denote an interdisciplinary criticism, not a pluralist concept. In a pluralistic universe, literature is the province of no single discipline. There is no pure isolable quality of "literariness" inside a piece of writing that awaits discovery by the critic, and by the critic alone, nor any essential truth to the object that forbids all approaches to it save one. Sociologists study literature as validly as literary critics do, just as literary critics study sociological materials as validly as sociologists do. Neither approach rules out the other, nor does it try to incorporate the other. Pluralism acknowledges that two descriptions using different concepts and methods may usefully apply to a phenomenon and not be comparable (compatible or contradictory). Sociologists study literature by constituting literature as a sociological object to be investigated sociologically. Since sociology does not use literary-nonliterary distinctions except in the most general sense, sociology levels literature with other social constructs. This is a reduction in the sense that sociology looks at literature from the same sociological standpoint that it looks at music, billboards, religious rituals, and so on. But it is not a reduction in that it does not rule out other interpretations of literature, nor does it claim a greater truth value for them except in terms of sociology.

A pluralist model of inquiry ensures a legitimate plurality of interpretations, a division of disciplines. On methodological grounds, its says that inquirers cannot perform literary interpretation and sociological interpretation at the same time. Just because *Moby-Dick*, for example, yields to literary description and sociological description does not mean that it yields to a fusion of both. Mixing descriptions entails mixing definitions, assumptions, aims, principles of selection and analysis, in a word, mixing methods. But how can one discuss a feature of *Moby-Dick*, say, its nautical language, in a literary way (as metaphor, allegory, etc.) at the same time that one discusses it in a sociological way (as evidence of the nature of nautical language in New England or merchant marine social structures and economic practices)? Both questions are important, but they cannot be answered simultaneously. To do so, one would have to begin with two distinct definitions of the text, one as a literary construct and the other as a sociological artifact. Since each definition solicits a different interpretative method, there is no way to proceed in the analysis and preserve both definitions. (To define a literary construct as a sociological artifact or vice versa is entirely valid, but from then on we have only one definition and its concomitant method.) So, pluralism says, when we cross disciplinary boundaries, when we break free of our attachment to traditional disciplinary material and enlarge our researches to include material from other disciplines or when we stick to our own material but implement another discipline's method, we must make a choice: either to treat the material disciplinarily defined as *this* (literature) and proceed with a corresponding methodology (literary analysis) or adopt the methods of the other discipline and define the material as *that*.

How does sociology of literature get around the pluralist impasse and reach an interdisciplinary stage? What are the methods and conventions which make sociology of literature more than just a standard sociological study of literary objects?

In the introduction to a special issue of *Critical Inquiry* on "The Sociology of Literature" (1988), the editors—Priscilla Parkhurst Ferguson, Philippe Desan, and Wendy Griswold—confess that sociology of literature has not clearly answered those questions. (A 1986 issue of *Critical Inquiry*, devoted to "Pluralism and Its Discontents," spells out pluralist debates and serves as an interesting foil to this issue.) Although they assert anti-pluralistically that "sociology does not constitute just one more approach to literature," that "a sociological practice is essential to literature" (421), Ferguson, Desan, and Griswold acknowledge its lack of "intellectual and institutional clarity" (421) and its "current disarray" (425). They note the disagreements among literary sociologists as to what their field actually is or does and they underscore the practitioners' resistance to disciplinary closure. The editors even admit that the "very term" that names the practice is "something of an oxymoron" (421), an admission bearing upon the humanities-social science incompatibility.

However, despite the disorganization and paradoxicality of sociology, the editors argue, sociology of literature still thrives as an exciting scholarly activity: "none of these limitations affects the vitality and rigor of the larger enterprise" (421—one might wonder how rigor and lack of clarity may coexist). The editors offer four justifications for this simultaneous vitality and disarray. Apart from asserting such trivial formulations as "literature and society necessarily explain one another" (421) and "[non-sociological theories of literature] join in a collective denial of the social and historical components of any text" (428), the editors legitimate sociology of literature by saying that the perceived confusions in it are due to: 1) a spurious theoretical-empirical distinction that sociologists rightly blur (423); 2) critics' adherence to "the disciplinary organization of universities and the ideological rigidities of schools of thought" (424); 3) "the conflicting traditions that are its intellectual heritage" (425—the traditions are romanticism, positivism, and Marxism); and 4) the academy's assumption of "an absolute division between material reality and intellectual activity" (428). The editors do not make arguments to support these assertions, nor do they give examples of ideological rigidities or absolute divisions of the material and intellectual sphere. They simply assume that these institutional limits exist and that sociology of literature should override them.

After noting first that sociology of literature is "not an established field or academic discipline" and that practitioners "subscribe to a wide range of theories and methods" (421), the authors proceed to affirm that such variety and field-heterogeneity is due to the "enormous gulf" between literary studies and sociology as traditionally defined. To exemplify this discrepancy, the editors focus on the practices' sharp terminological differences.

Literary critics look at *works*, *texts*, *writers*, and *readers*. They speculate about the *creation*, *reception*, and *interpretations* of literature. Social scientists, on the other hand, discuss *books* and literary *institutions* and dwell upon the *production*, *distribution*, and *consumption* of cultural *products*. (422)

The authors continue with a cautious and ambivalent discussion about the institutional viability of sociology of literature as a successful academic enterprise. However, in this list of contrasting terms, the authors also (and perhaps unintentionally) indicate a methodological problem in the strategy, especially in regard to "the interdisciplinary nature of the sociology of literature" (424). That is: how can an inquiry address literary objects as both "texts" and as "books"? If I say "*Moby-Dick* is a text," then I commit myself to all the propositions entailed by this statement, those entailments specified by the other words in the editors' literary list. These include "*Moby-Dick* is comprised of a play of semiotic differences," "the interpretation of the novel should correspond to the writer's creation of it or readers' reception of it," "the work means something." In these cases, a literary methodology follows that involves "speculation" upon the textual meaning, the speculation bearing either upon writer's creation or reader's reception. In the writer-text-reader circuit we witness a circulation of meaning that literary criticism proposes to describe. The novel at the center of this interpretative process is a hermeneutical text with literary characteristics, and a hermeneutical method isolating those characteristics is called for.

But if I say "*Moby-Dick* is a book," then I commit myself to wholly disparate (though not contradictory) propositions. Again, with the other words in the sociological list as guides, we can include among the entailed propositions: "*Moby-Dick* is a material good," "the novel is institutionally manifested," "presses and distributors and consumers control its circulation," "the book has meaning as a cultural product." In these cases, a sociological method follows that involves empirical research into the organizations and economics of publishing, advertising, and popular reading habits. In the producer-book-consumer circuit we witness a circulation of products that sociological analysis proposes to describe. The novel at the center of this social process is a sociological commodity with literary characteristics and a sociological method isolating those characteristics is called for.

These two approaches do not exclude one another, but because they cannot in their present form entail one another, there is no way to combine them into one coherent inquiry. Or rather, the entailments of the "text" attribution and the entailments of the "book" attribution do not converge. The conceptual complex shaping literary study (text, writer, reader, intention, interpretation, speculation) has no room for the conceptual complex shaping sociological study (book, distribution, consumption, product) and vice versa. The concept "text" demands speculative criticism and the concept "book" demands empirical fact-finding. We have here not only a logical implication where one concept implies another, but a methodological implication, where one concept implies a particular method. In both cases, literary analysis of literature and sociological analysis of literature do not substantially interact (although they may complement and corroborate one another).

This is not to say that the revision and reconstruction of an interpretative complex like literary criticism into a sociology of literature is impossible. The relations and entailments of all the constituents of a methodological structure need not be considered an absolute totality with pure and rigid boundaries. However, if we do decide to alter the structures of our inquiries, if we wish to redefine subject matters and reorganize concepts, we must do so circumspectly, with an awareness of the relations and entailments of the things we revise. For sociologists read sociologically, historians historically, and so on not only because of institutional training and conditioning but also because of the common need for methodological coherence. If interpretive limits were due only to institutional causes, then we might be able to decide on purely institutional grounds that we should change our practices. But there are coherence and consistency criteria that obtain as well. A sociological study of literature emerges in a sociological institution, but it also emerges through a coordinated set of sociological concepts and practices. As we cross disciplinary boundaries, we cross not only institutional structures but also methodological structures. Unless the latter are accounted for in any large-scale modification of inquiry, the results will prove inconsistent and unclear, nor will we know how to apply proper criteria to them.

This is to say that each discipline may use the results of the other, but only after the one has recontextualized the other's results within the one's methodological complex. There is always the temptation to say that the other discipline gets the object wrong, that sociology of literature reduces the work's specific literariness to general social processes. But the literary critic cannot in any way support the claim that literary criticism's literariness is intrinsic or essential to the text while "historicality" or "sociologicality" and so on rest only in the historian's or sociologist's activity. All the literary critic can say is that he or she reads the text as literature and that this approach is in some way distinct from the other critics' approach and for some purposes better. For the text itself cannot serve as a sufficient criterion to determine which approach is better, to assess, of the literary critic's or the historian's interpretations, which is more true. That is a pragmatic issue not residing in the object itself.

The methodological distinctions and pluralist consequences of this argument are what an interdisciplinary inquiry like sociology of literature countervails. Sociology of literature does not fail the test of conceptual coherence; it defies it. As the *Critical Inquiry* editors concede, the interdisciplinarity of sociology of literature remains in a state of "inevitable variation," with "disagreements among its proponents" (430) preventing any sharp determination of its purviews and strategies. But this institutional chaos is a strategy of resistance, not a methodological washout. Clear conceptual lines drawn between one terminology and another, clear methodological fences raised between empirical and speculative, classification and valuation, and set divisions of data and ideas, texts and contexts, literature and society—sociology of literature traverses them all, and for a calculated reason. The diverse practices comprising the program "cross basic divisions within the contemporary intellectual field" and are "subject to constant reformulation. . . . In consequence, disciplinary boundaries seem less rigid, less logical, less authoritative than ever before" (422). The disarray of sociology of literature is a planned disorder designed to subvert the power of institutionalized intellectual distinctions. Its tenebrous interdisciplinarity is a critique of precise disciplinarity. The fusion term "sociology of literature" gains its currency strictly through its oppositional meaning, namely, "against disciplinary distinction." Its affirmations are cloudy, but its negation of disciplinarity is resolute.

theory   Theoretical research and training reached its height in the late 1970s and by the mid-1980s was beginning to decline in professional prestige. The deaths of Roland Barthes, Lacan, de Man, and Foucault, the anti-theoretical arguments leveled by neopragmatists in the early '80s, the discovery of de Man's wartime writings and the re-examination of Heidegger's nazism, the wearisome repetitiveness and poor quality of much second generation theoretical work—all conspired to dethrone critical theory, to render it *passé*. The philosophical rigor and conceptual inventiveness theory claimed for itself often proved unfounded when literary critics' theoretical speculations were set alongside related arguments made by logicians and analytic philosophers. Also, theoretical practices were too much restricted to 1960s and '70s academic reading practices to survive '80s changes in the academy (tightening budgets, emphasis on undergraduate education, attacks from William Bennett, Lynne Cheney, and others on the right, the advent of identity politics). Theory now belongs to intellectual history. Although one often sees theoretical propositions popping up in political criticism, cultural studies, interdisciplinary debates, and discussions of race and gender, the statements are usually reduced to the status of given premises. The critic does not raise the theoretical point in order to explore it or to build a method upon it. Instead, the point gives the critic a quick point of departure, an heuristic angle on the material being interpreted. The term "theory" now signifies anything non-empirical, conceptual, or abstract. One uses it when one wishes to sound non-empirical, conceptual, or abstract.

voice   The word "voice" has a dual significance in contemporary criticism, one personal and one political. In its personal reference, "voice" signifies those responses and expressions unique to every human psyche. This voice comes from the self, from the memories, feelings, and beliefs residing in a core of personal identity. While most communications owe their form and purpose to conventional rules of speech and writing, voice accords primarily with a structure of personal experience, though it must obviously assume communicable form. Because the experiential contents and habits of selfhood necessarily vary from person to person, by remaining true to its motivation, voice becomes the surest sign of individuality, the clearest evidence of a self's singularity. Voice is not just a speaking subject's utterance. It is a particular subject's vision of the world, her outlook on things, her elemental registration of what happens. In voice one finds personalized effects of cultural processes, political systems, and social events, limited but authentic evidence of historical reality. Voice is unmistakable. It is not *the* truth, but it is the truth of this or that experience of this or that phenomenon. This is why critics who wish to explain various historical phenomena will often turn to voice as its interpretative key, for the phenomena are best understood through a human subject's apprehension of it. The truth of occurrences rests in the unmediated vocalization of them.

In its political reference, "voice" signifies not a personal experience, but a political position. To have a voice in this sense means to have political meaning, to be admitted to the political marketplace. Voice represents an opinion, not an experience. The subjective determinants underlying a personal voice here become political conditions that direct the voice and that voice in turn announces. The opinion voice carries may ultimately stem from personal experience, but if so, that experience has political parameters. The experiential basis of a political voice differs from one person to another because of political differences shaping the experience and the persons themselves. Political voice differences come from differences in race, class, gender, region, religion, and nationality, all of which are interpreted as political effects. Blacks and whites, rich and poor, men and women, Jews and non-Jews, Southerners and Northerners, and so on will all necessarily have different voices and their contrasts will have a political meaning. Indeed, those contrasts will often serve as an index both of familiar political environments as they work on different individuals and groups and of implicit ideological oppressions persons profit by and suffer from. Scholars who wish to outline those differences and effects will, then, focus upon political voices as a form of historical exposure, a clarification of actual political realities and an acknowledgment of those voices repressed by them.

Both these references for "voice" critics find worthwhile and useful. They investigate this or that personal voice by pursuing conventional biographical scholarship and compiling all of the factual information, private circumstances, and emotional factors shaping the person's voice. They investigate this or that political voice by pursuing conventional historical scholarship and piecing together all the socioeconomic causes, group identifications, and political commitments constituting the spokesperson's voice. The advantage of the personal reference is that it sets clear research parameters for an historical inquiry. A personal voice interpretation limits itself to the experienced reality of the vocalizer. Historical material is filtered through the psyche of one person. Historical evidence is reduced to that person's voice. Since the interpretation makes no broad historical claims beyond the personal context, its partiality

does not threaten its validity. The advantage of the political reference is that it fulfills representational goals that the personal reference does not. A political voice interpretation reaches beyond
the personal experience of one person's voice to account for the
sociopolitical conditions that shape that voice. A political voice ar-
ticulates political circumstances and represents political constitu-
encies. Whereas the personal voice tends to lapse into biography,
personality, humanism, or a politically inconsequential privacy, the
political voice eschews the seductions of ego and maintains a forceful, trans-individual political critique, engages with rival political,
not personal positions on a critical battleground.

These argumentative goods are obviously serviceable to criticism, but they are also distinct. Though personal and political
modify the same word, "voice," the meanings and methods that go
with each one are unmixable. One may not validly carry out personal and political voice investigations at the same time. Voice may
not refer to personal self and political position simultaneously.
Whereas a personal voice springs from a singular unique psyche, a
political voice derives from a political situation that those inhabiting it all share. The former meaning excludes the latter and the
latter subsumes the former. In choosing a personal reference for
"voice," one contemplates a unique subjective realm where feeling, memory, sensation, and will preside. Whatever lies outside the
self becomes mere experiential material, phenomenal contents the
self assumes an inimitable attitude toward. Although political realities certainly affect the personal self, they do so only as the contents
of an individual's waking life, as experiences absorbed by the self
and interpreted in personal terms. If one asserts that political en-
virons actually determine the internal nature of the self, then one
has thereby substituted meanings, has traded a personal voice reference for a political voice reference. The personal self and the
personal voice in that context have a political basis, one that makes
all ostensibly personal characteristics fundamentally political constructs that model individuals into political effects, group representatives. This is not a combination of the two voices, but a
redefinition of the personal in terms of the political. We have lost
the former reference. As soon as we enter a conceptual framework
where all subjective entities have political origins, the personal
voice becomes a political statement—not a personal statement
that has political implications, but a political perspective from the

very start. There is no more pre-political inner space for voice to emerge from.

However, despite the conceptual incompatibility of personal voice and political voice, one often finds in contemporary critical practice a fusion of the two. Critics using the word occasionally like to play on both references. For example, in speaking of "The African Writer and the English Language" (first published in 1975, but recently republished in a postcolonial anthology), Chinua Achebe writes,

> What I do see is a new voice coming out of Africa, speaking of African experience in a world-wide language. . . . The African writer should aim to use English in a way that brings out his message best without altering the language to the extent that its value as a medium of international exchange will be lost. He should aim at fashioning out an English which is at once universal and able to carry his peculiar experience. (433)

Achebe's "voice" can preserve a general "African experience" and one person's "peculiar experience." Voice can have political implications as a "medium of international exchange" ("universal" here means "transcontinental") and personal implications as "his message" (equated in the next paragraph with one African writer's "evocation of his bizarre world"). Exactly how "voice" can do both, how "voice" can represent an African writer's personal self and a generic African situation, Achebe leaves unstated. Perhaps some fuzzy proposition about African writers' capacity to singularize their expressions but maintain a "world-wide language" is embedded in Achebe's personal-political alloy, but any demonstration of it is missing.

However, that absence of distinction or, rather, confusion of voices proves useful. For the advantages of fusing personal-political polarities are considerable, especially for critics enmeshed in identity politics, because each meaning buttresses the other. First, the personal dimension gives to a political interpretation of voice an irrefutability: if a political opinion rests upon experienced facts, how can one confute it? Second, the political dimension grants a personal interpretation of voice a relevance: if a personal utterance has positive political associations, how can one limit it to individualistic bounds? In the first case, a political opinion becomes an indisputable fact, individuals' direct, but generalized response to things that happen to them. In the second case, a personal expression becomes a normative representation of historical conditions, not just one person's perspective on things. The term thereby possesses a firm truth and a broad applicability. It both respects the certitude of individual experience and recognizes the conditioning of political reality.

Of course, in doing so the dual meaning usage jumbles discordant concepts. "Voice" may refer smoothly to response to personal experience or to representation of political identity, but it cannot do both without mixing mutually exclusive concepts. The self of the former reference is contrary to the self of the latter reference. The subjective region of the former ousts the political variables of the latter, while the historical circumstances of the latter infiltrate the personality of the former. The concepts do not match and cannot match. One may alternate them, but not logically unite them.

But no matter. The conceptual objection to personal-political unity pales before the usage's rhetorical and political benefits. The personal side guarantees the authenticity of the reference: this voice is *this* person's voice, and nobody can gainsay its truth. The political side proves the representativeness of the reference: this voice is a group viewpoint, and nobody can deny it a place in the contest of political agencies. The double use garners both benefits, and in an intellectual context riddled with equations like "the personal is political," the confusion is a virtue.

what so-and-so calls   A certain mode of citation has cropped up in criticism recently, a type of allusion whose novelty and frequency bears some analysis. This is the "what so-and-so calls *x*" gesture, the reference to some other scholar's or philosopher's name for a social, discursive, or textual phenomenon. The citation usually follows a critic's short description of some historical or textual particular and functions as a generalization of it. The critic will note something that happens in a novel, or recount some specific social condition relevant to the text at hand, or relate some theoretical maneuver previous critics have worked upon the text, and then position it as an instance of . . . well, of "what so-and-so calls *x*." In other words, citation replaces definition. Allusion renders a fuller description unnecessary. Instead of delineating what it is, critics say offhand what others have called it and leave it at that.

Here are some examples, these taken from recent issues of *PMLA*:

Specifically, [Harriet Wilson] risked undermining what Houston A. Baker, Jr., calls "the New England ideal so frequently appearing in Afro-American narratives," that of "free, dignified, and individualistic labor." (Ernest, 430)

One way of interpreting both the history of modern colonialism and the specificity of our postcolonial condition is to pay close attention to what we, like Luis Brandaon, might call our various "scruples." (Mohanty, 108)

Periodization seems to have won the most hostility by facilitating professional "identity cards" that define obligatory units of academic initiation and professional credentialling (and that manifest what Mary Poovey calls, in another context, "the involuntary periodicity of the reproductive system." (Robbins, 40)

In an age increasingly concerned with sociability, gentlemen were eager to derive from the company of women what Carol Kay calls "the prestige of civilized sensitivity." (Potkay, 121)

. . . I also claim that Rilke's poetry constitutes not only a parallel to Baudelaire's, as Paul de Man believes, but what one, adapting a term from Barbara Johnson, might call a "third Baudelairean revolution." (Ryan, 1129)

In revising the boundaries of what has traditionally constituted the folklore text, recent scholars . . . have reconceptualized the distinctions between textual representations and what Robert Georges calls "complex communicative events." (Blount, 583)

Why are these allusions included? Why does the critic not use his or her own words? What do they provide that an original description would not? How do they work in the sentences?

In each example, the critic rounds out a strong assertion by resorting to someone else's label. The "what so-and-so calls *x*" phrase adds a clarifying reference, supporting the rest of the sentence with a pithy, yet loaded epithet. In the interest of scholarly communication, one assumes, the critic borrows another's authoritative phrase and tacks it on to his own phrasing, collegially aligning his interpretation with the other's. The only originality of the assertion itself lies in the critic's connection of this particular subject matter with that cited critic's general term. The general term serves as a supplement to the critic's isolation of some textual or historical fact, an accessory judgment that somehow and to some extent unveils the fact's significance. Presumably, the allusion supplies a terminology that situates the particular within a collateral but illuminating context.

However, in doing so, the "what so-and-so calls *x*" formula does not enhance an explicit definition or description of the labeled phenomena. It substitutes for them. In the above passages, the cited calls terminate the representation of the thing at hand. Little empirical information or logical analysis follows. The commentary smoothly proceeds to other issues, as if the critic's identification of a thing that some critical authority has given a label to sufficiently characterizes the thing. The critics argue as if the citation distinguishes the thing adequately enough so that further analysis is not required. However, a denomination does not describe, define, or portray what it names. A name, particularly one openly lifted from another context (as in the Robbins and Ryan quotations), does not determine what the named thing is, how it works, what its components are, what it means. It adds no specific information about the object. Obviously, the term "x" has been derived from historical data, texts, or theories and now plays a classifying role in criticism (as these examples show). But a classification does nothing more than include in or exclude from the class any particular that comes its way. And it treats the particulars only in respect to the predicates on which the class is formed. Therefore, if we wish to understand the phenomenon called x as more than simply something inside or outside a class, then our representations of it must involve more than the phrase "what so-and-so calls x." If we wish to understand texts and events in their complexity and singularity, we must not let the designation of them replace an empirical or logical investigation.

Although these citations are posed as clarifications, in fact they function more as circumlocutions. Certainly, any reference to a related interpretation, one that has produced an edifying name for the object under consideration, may favor the argument. The reference may give readers more clues as to what conceptual framework obtains in the discussion. But in the absence of thorough and patient inquiry into the immediate subject, such references raise more questions than they answer. For example: does the name really apply here? The critic quoting it posits its relevance, but does not bother to ponder if or how the call can validly be pulled from one context and inserted into another. Such a cursory and cute reference leaves no room to ask whether Harriet Wilson's concept of "the New England ideal" matches that of Houston Baker. Does Luis Brandaon (writing in 1610) mean by "scruples" the same thing we mean by the word "scruples"? Does "the involuntary periodicity of the reproductive system" have anything to do with professional "periodization"? What exactly? A pat declaration that such-and-such is an instance of what so-and-so calls x merely begs the question of how so? In what way?

Another question the citation raises: is the label itself correct? Was it correctly inferred from the phenomena it purports to encapsulate? Presumably, the critic invoking the term knows the genesis of it, where and how it was arrived at, but those details are omitted. The implication is that the term carries its authority within itself, not in its just correspondence to a state of affairs, and so its mere mention sufficiently justifies it. It enjoys an already established legitimacy, and so any further explanation of it is unnecessary. Such a casual yet positive reference renders the term or phrase unassailable. The brevity of its appearance prevents readers from appraising its propriety. The only information accompanying the term is the name of its originator. Apparently, because a more or less noted scholar coined the term, it possesses accuracy and validity. To the phrase "what so-and-so calls x," one might respond, "Was that so irresistible a description?" Until the label receives some substantiating evidence or specifying commentary, readers can only wonder what they are supposed to gather from it.

One final question the citation raises: what does the label mean? The label is supposed to summarize the phenomena under deliberation, to designate its general import. But what does the label itself import? What is a "complex communicative event"? What is "the prestige of civilized sensitivity"? Ideally, these terms clarify the more or less intricate social entity being expounded in the argument, but in fact the terms themselves warrant clarification. They are too conceptually dense and abstract to signify plainly. Except for "scruples," each label cited above is a composite of concepts, and the "what so-and-so calls x" gesture explains neither the conceptual pieces nor their principle of composition. (The semantic difficulty with "scruples" is not one of complexity, but of philology—what "scruples" means in 1610—and of pragmatics—how "scruples" is used in Brandaon's comments on the licitness of the slave trade.) The term "prestige of civilized sensitivity" conjoins three concepts into a vaguely causal relation: "sensitivity" of a "civilized" kind grants "prestige" to those perceived as possessing it. Conceding the fairly untroubled meaning of "prestige" and "civilized," one still might wonder what "sensitivity" here denotes. Obviously, it means "a capacity of being sensitive," but "sensitive" could refer to, among other things, a delicate awareness of others' feelings and experiences, a heightened susceptibility to all forms of sensation, or an acute understanding of tricky situations, of sensitive matters. Does this "sensitivity" extend to all things or just to certain things? The predicate "civilized" narrows down the sense of "sensitivity," but only by presupposing a tacit distinction: "civilized sensitivity" as opposed to "uncivilized sensitivity." What the latter signifies and exactly why the former has "prestige" and the latter does not remains unexplained.

The original context of the term may resolve all these questions, but a simple mention of the term in another context does not. The term's citation does not prove or demonstrate or refine or clarify the point. On the contrary, in introducing unsubstantiated neologisms of questionable derivation, in opting for references filled with semantic perplexities, in neglecting to explain the meaning of the reference or the reason for its citation, critics using the "what so-and-so calls x" tag impede straightforward communication of ideas and evidence. The addendum provides a scholar's name and a catchy label—that is all. What the addendum produces are problems of context, questions of sense and relevance, a surfeit of generality.

If the "what so-and-so calls x" gesture does not answer any of these semantic and empirical questions, why do critics indulge the pseudo-argumentative habit? Well, precisely in order to evade those questions. In citing a noted critic's term instead of extending their own descriptions, critics skirt the need to gather evidence, to summon premises, to complete their analyses. The citation serves as a mini-argument from authority. A symptom of group thinking, it indicates the failure of scholars to think for themselves, to develop their own points, to think through the issues and research the material until they have acquired enough erudition and know-how to compose their own descriptions and draw their own conclusions. And the reassuring glow that accompanies such on-the-run, in-the-know, cliquish references offsets the scholar's own insecurity, the individual or professional anxiety that finds its refuge in whatever institutional group happens to grant it appeasement. The "what so-and-so calls x" catchphrase flatters the famous and ratifies the novitiate. It is a quick road to professional membership.

Epilogue

The preceding discussions of critical terms all operate on a basic premise: the significance of a term rests on the role it plays in a critical method. On this assumption, the analyses have sought to divine a continuity of usage in scholarly practice, in this case, a strategically anti-disciplinary, consistently inconsistent style of academic expression. The goal has been to clarify these terms' customary institutional and political uses, given that their traditional methodological uses are confused and random. For, despite the breakdown of literary study as a discipline, it has survived as a profession. It must harbor orderliness somewhere, must have some regular procedures that allow it to retain its institutional identity. Even if these are squarely anti-methodological, scholars and teachers must communicate them in such a way that other scholars may repeat them and students may learn them. Unless it satisfies the transmissibility requirement, a scholarly practice cannot thrive. Unless the terms of an interpretation have a recognizable place and purpose in an overall critical method, its audience will be hard pressed to identify the terms clearly, to know what criteria to apply to them. Unless one can point to a particular interpretation and say, "Here is where and why so-and-so brings in this or that concept" or "the scholar turns to this phrase at this moment because . . . ," the interpretation remains inert, unreadable from a methodological standpoint. Unless one can take the interpretation's fundamental terms and show how and where they typically function in an inquiry, the interpretation has no consistent use value.

This methodological requirement of transmissibility applies only to scholarly institutions, not to the arts, politics, or ordinary social behavior. The point is that the advent of new terms and their place in new interpretative postures has institutional value only if they aim toward a methodological status. If innovations in inquiry and disputations of set categories and canons are themselves to become part of a scholarly endeavor, then they must assume a standard form, one that can be institutionalized into research projects, classroom demonstrations, and an evaluative measure. Now, such institutionalizations in the academy rely on the exclusion, division, compartmentalization of history, society, and persons. But those practices also provide a discipline with focus and consistency, with the kind of methodological integrity that will allow persons to recognize it, to enter it with confidence, to understand it clearly as a discrete region of inquiry with its own rules and designs. Having learned the field limits of their situation, inquirers within a methodological framework know what counts as an object of study, what terminology properly applies to it, what conclusions may be legitimately drawn from it. And the more precise the limits, the more effective the inquiries will be. We may be wary of specific practices and the exclusions they entail and revise them if we find them unacceptable, but we must also recognize that they serve pragmatic purposes, that they are valid first on pragmatic grounds, not on the basis of their truth or representational accuracy. We may find that this or that practice misrepresents nature and history or that it is politically undesirable or morally wrong, but such practices, if well developed, also organize a set of terms, contents, and attitudes into a recognizable terrain of inquiry. If some argument, evidence, or theory exposes that practice as false or repugnant, then the practice should go. But then, also, the new material must replace it with a new organization, a new terminology and a new method that scholars and students may adapt to and carry out on their own.

This is why one can often understand and assess a discipline and its changes by observing the forms of training it develops. By looking at methods course syllabi, by noting what teachers in the field identify as their common subject matter, what kinds of terms, arguments, and evidence fulfill their class assignments, what standards they apply to students' work, what kinds of dissertations they ask students to write, we get to know what is the shape of the discipline. In the training of aspiring professionals, even at the undergraduate level, we see what knowledges and what skills get transmitted, what contents and behaviors characterize the discipline over time. In asking what procedures persist in critical practice, however much its contents and goals change and however logically fallacious and empirically weak the procedures are, we understand best what the practice is. The introduction of neophytes to disciplinary (or counterdisciplinary) methods is a useful index of a discipline's nature and extent.

It is therefore no surprise that the broad transformations in the meaning and practice of literary criticism have been reflected in the variations in literary critical training that have occurred over the last decades. It has been remarkable how quickly seemingly remote and high-level changes in scholarly movements, in esoteric theories, in other fields like psychoanalysis and anthropology, and in political imperatives have filtered down through graduate programs and on into undergraduate classrooms. Indeed, if one were to compare a typical literature class forty years ago with one today, it might seem that even though the works studied sometimes are the same, the differences in what was said about those works and what approach was taken to them would outnumber the resemblances. As proof of this generalization, consider the recent curricular changes of advanced literary study.

Forty years ago, students immersed themselves in a literary and cultural history, reading and researching until they had acquired a broad erudition and could call themselves specialists in some slice of the tradition. They added to this historical contextualization the skill of formal textual explication (though they did not always bring the two processes into alliance). Professionalism entailed a working knowledge of European and American literature and culture plus a thorough familiarity with the writers specialized in, with their works and lives, with the historical contexts and formal structures of their writings. At the end of their studies, students were expected to be conversant with Plato, Dante, Shakespeare, Rousseau, and the rest and expert in, say, the editorial difficulties of Whitman's *Leaves of Grass* or the metaphorical complications of Pope's *Dunciad*. Henceforth, their role as professors and critics lay in imparting to future students the literary tradition they had spent years assimilating and the practical analysis they had mastered. In that way, they trained future students to become scholars like themselves.

Twenty years ago, students surveyed the schools of interpretation then arriving from the Continent, choosing among the deconstruction of Jacques Derrida, the psychoanalysis of Jacques Lacan, the historicism of Michel Foucault, and the various Marxisms and Feminisms then coming to prominence the thinking most congenial to students' interests. They added to this absorption of theoretical approaches a formal skill of theoretical explication of texts, of revealing a text's theoretical complexities and problematizations. Professionalism consisted of a savvy facility in implementing these theories, in applying them to this or that text in accordance with the master's precepts. Upon completing their studies, students were supposed to produce, say, a Derridean reading of most any literary work, their skill at doing so being measured by how acutely the fledgling critics handled a Derridean textual strategy. Henceforth, their role as professors and critics lay in introducing future students to the variety of theoretical approaches and showing them how to reproduce them in their own interpretations. That way, they trained students to become theorists like themselves.

Today, here is what training in literary criticism involves. Students begin a cursory study of a cultural tradition but then proceed to address political and institutional questions accompanying that study, questions such as "Who composed that tradition?" and "What groups profit by it and what groups are excluded from it?" That is, they begin with a cultural tradition not as a set of facts and texts to be immersed in, but as an institution itself to be analyzed. The institutionalization is precisely the object of description. Professionalism requires that one abandon any assumptions of disinterestedness or empirical purity and maintain an abiding cognizance of the powers and interests shaping humanist knowledge. The knowledge itself, be it empirical knowledge of names, dates, events, periods, plots, characters, and poems, or practical skills of explication, editing, composition, and interpretation, matters less than the sociopolitical framework within which that knowledge has meaning and value. Upon completing their studies, students are expected to understand their discipline as a political construct, to articulate not a scholarly field but a politics of humanist inquiry. Henceforth, their role as professors and critics lies in inculcating this institutional awareness, in exposing students to all the power relations making up a culture (these being structured largely by race, class, and gender). Thereby, they train students to become political speculators and cultural commentators.

To get a clearer picture of these distinctions and how the concept of transmissibility applies to them, consider what kind of coursework falls into each category. In a scholarly time, students took courses in literary criticism in order to develop some *humanitas*, some cultural consciousness that might shape their sensibilities and deepen their understanding. Exposure to the literary monuments of the past gave to students an aesthetic sense and a historical sense, a feel for tradition, chronology, invention, and taste. Forms, ideas, and values individuals encountered could then be allied to different texts, authors, and epochs, ordered by the sequence of Western thought and imagination as they were manifested in literary language.

It was the task of a curriculum to supply this history of ideas and artworks. So, for example, a course on British Romanticism would focus on the relevant artistic, philosophical, and political themes (organic form, individualism, anti-reason, revolution) and explore their instantiation in Blake, Wordsworth, Byron, etc. A class lecture on Wordsworth might commence with his *Lyrical Ballads* and their portrayal of rural life and of nature, relating those concerns to the poet's upbringing, to his anti-urbanism, to the ballad genre and its social connotations. The lecture might conclude with a treatment of *The Prelude*, Wordsworth's epic about his own early life, invoking ideas of selfhood, memory, biography, and epic genre and recounting events in the French Revolution in order to explain the poem's import. Students would leave the class with a general familiarity with Wordsworth's thinking and with his poetics. The relations between Wordsworth's poetic practice and Alexander Pope's, between the type of redemption found in Milton's *Paradise Lost* and that found in *The Prelude*, would begin to make sense and would become ever more explicit as students took more classes and filled in gaps in their knowledge of the tradition.

In a theoretical era, students took courses in literary criticism in order to acquire a knowledge that forms an important, but narrow subset of *humanitas*: interpretative sophistication. Courses imparted to students not a historical sense or an aesthetic discrimination, but rather a conceptual acuity. Exposure to the complex methods of analysis proposed by Derrida, Lacan, Foucault et al. gave to students powerful tools of interpretation, a handy set of concepts with which to break texts down into their fundamental structures. Theorists of art, literature, and language taught students to appreciate relations between form and content, words and meanings, and text and text in a novel hypercritical way. In class lectures, empirical knowledge of literary history was set aside for a problematizing discussion of the very notion of a literary history. The application of aesthetic distinctions such as generic ones to a work of art gave way to a reflection upon the category of genre per se. A class lecture on Wordsworth would forgo biographical and thematic considerations and instead select one poem like "A Slumber Did My Spirit Seal" and, with the poem serving as a pretext, rehearse a series of theoretical axioms. Students would leave the class conceiving Wordsworth as the site of theoretical cruxes. The point was not to gather information about Wordsworth or his corpus, but to use Wordsworth as an occasion for honing interpretative skills.

In today's political climate, whether they know it or not, students take courses in literary criticism in order to experience political enlightenment. The insight they enjoy amounts to this: all modes of evaluation, decision-making, adjudication, inclusion and exclusion, etc., most of which claim logical, aesthetic, or scientific grounds as their criteria of judgment, ultimately come down to power contests between rival groups. The traditional incorporation of this material as the best of what was thought and said by humanity is simply the culmination of a political ideology, the last concealment of the politics of Western man. Within this historical drama, works of art, literature, and philosophy created by those in group A (men, whites, etc.) stand as rationalizations, *apologias*, or outright misrepresentations of the ways group A has subordinated group B (women, minorities, etc.) and sustained its privilege. Works created by those in group B stand as indirect or subversive exposures of and protests against the subordinating acts group A has tried to hide. To appreciate properly that counter-tradition, classroom pedagogy begins by converting formalist and non-political thematic interpretation into a relentless political criticism. Students are instructed to take a work and identify its representation of groups, its exemplifications of them in images, characters, speech, and plot. Then, with the political framework in hand, students assign the text a value, assess its social conscience and its moral bearings. In reconnecting literary and artistic representations to political truths, students begin to comprehend the workings of power and subjugation in Western society. This is the moral imperative of literary criticism and of much humanities teaching today.

So, faithful to its liberal *ethos*, the liberal arts now assume a new social role: to reveal systematic processes of repression in Western civilization, to recuperate lives, voices, and texts the group A tradition has suppressed, to expose racist, sexist, and homophobic discourses for exactly what they are. It is the job of a humanities curriculum to supply the raw material for this kind of diagnosis. Humanities courses offer texts for study that suit the requirements of political interpretation, both non-canonical texts heretofore neglected and canonical texts henceforth recontextualized within political issues. Wordsworth is still taught, but his import lies not in the facts of his life and practice as a Romantic poet or in the representational problems of his expressivist poetics. Class discussions now single out a felicitous political element in his work, for example, his treatment of women, and infer an ideology from it. "A Slumber Did My Spirit Seal" and the other Lucy poems are interpreted as patriarchal utterances, as masculine self-absorption disguised as a sensitive lament over a lost love. Students leave the class fully aware of the sexist parameters of Wordsworth's personal attitudes (which are representative of his culture). Other classes students attend provide similar political lessons, recounting other versions of domination, pseudo-justification, and authentic protest until students graduate with a thoroughgoing sensitivity to power politics. That is the competence a literary criticism degree today signifies.

It makes perfect sense, then, that the terminology of literary criticism should now function precisely according to the rules of power politics. Therein lies the method of contemporary parlance. Obviously, for a practice to last, to gain institutional strength, to attract followers, it must possess a measure of regularity—but not necessarily an intellectual or logical regularity. This is what cultural studies, political criticism, and interdisciplinarity have realized. Notwithstanding its methodological failings, contemporary criticism still observes some form of consistency, but the consistency lies in acts of orienting inquiries and inquirers in certain political, anti-institutional directions. Criticism claims inquiry status, but bases its claim on a routine set of rhetorical-political gestures, not on rules of evidence and inference. No longer do terms certify their wielders' intellectual skills. No longer do they serve to establish evidence, to advance arguments, to discriminate amongst forms, to establish disciplinary identities. Instead, the usage of critical terms takes the form of a political induction. When a critic employs "cultural studies," "rethinking," "what so-and-so calls x," and so on, the critic does not proceed with a logical or empirical method of literary and cultural analysis. Rather, the critic assumes a political standing (cultural critic, epistemological prophet, etc.) and joins a select organization. The terms provide the critic with an institutional membership pass, even though many of the terms are ostensibly directed against institutions. They fulfill admissions standards to conference panels, to journal advisory boards, to shortlists for jobs. As political markers, not logical or empirical designations, they displace methodological criteria and shield critics from logical and empirical refutation. Current usage shows that criticism is not about knowledge of objects, but about the politics of inquiry, which includes the political status of the inquirer. Literary study is no longer literary analysis. It is now an occasion for institutional certification. Those who use terms in the right way display their intellectual discernment, their cultural interest, their political sensitivity, and their moral regard, which is to say, their eligibility for entering today's academic order. Critical terms are the tokens of belonging.

Bibliography

Achebe, Chinua. "The African Writer and the English Language." In *Colonial Discourse and Post-Colonial Theory: A Reader*, edited by Patrick Williams and Laura Chrisman. New York: Columbia University Press, 1994, 428–34.

Babha, Homi K. *The Location of Culture*. London and New York: Routledge, 1994.

Bergner, Gwen. "Who Is That Masked Woman? or, The Role of Gender in Fanon's *Black Skin, White Masks*." *PMLA* 110 (1995), 75–88.

Bernheimer, Charles. "Degas's Brothels: Voyeurism and Ideology." *Representations* 20 (1987), 158–86.

Blount, Marcellus. "The Preacherly Text: African-American Poetry and Vernacular Performance." *PMLA* 107 (1992), 582–93.

Boone, Joseph A., and Michael Cadden, editors. *Engendering Men: The Question of Male Feminist Criticism*. New York: Routledge, 1990.

Bové, Paul. *Mastering Discourse: The Politics of Intellectual Culture*. Durham, NC: Duke University Press, 1992.

Brantlinger, Patrick. *Crusoe's Footprints: Cultural Studies in Britain and America*. New York: Routledge, 1990.

Brenkman, John. *Culture and Domination*. Ithaca, NY and London: Cornell University Press, 1987.

Bromwich, David. *Politics by Other Means: Higher Education and Group Thinking*. New Haven, CT and London: Yale University Press, 1992.

Brooks, Cleanth. *The Well-Wrought Urn: Studies in the Structure of Poetry*. New York: Harcourt Brace, 1947.

Buell, Lawrence. "Melville and the Question of American Decolonization." *American Literature* 64 (1992), 215–37.

Butler, Judith. *Gender Trouble: Feminism and the Subversion of Identity*. New York: Routledge, 1990.

———. "Contingent Foundations: Feminism and the Question of 'Postmodernism.'" In *Critical Encounters: Reference and Responsibility in Deconstructive Writing*, edited by Cathy Caruth and Deborah Esch. New Brunswick, NJ: Rutgers University Press, 1995, 213–32.

Cascardi, Anthony, editor. *Literature and the Question of Philosophy*. Baltimore: Johns Hopkins University Press, 1987.

Clifford, James. *The Predicament of Culture: Twentieth-Century Ethnography, Literature, and Art.* Cambridge, MA and London: Harvard University Press, 1988.

Cornell, Drucilla. "Rethinking the Beyond Within the Real (Response to Rasch)." *Cultural Critique* 30 (1995), 223–34.

Davis, Mike. "Urban Renaissance and the Spirit of Postmodernism." *New Left Review* 151 (1985), 106–13.

de Man, Paul. *Allegories of Reading: Figural Language in Rousseau, Nietzsche, Rilke, and Proust.* New Haven, CT and London: Yale University Press, 1979.

———. *The Resistance to Theory.* Minneapolis: University of Minnesota Press, 1986.

Derrida, Jacques, "Différance." In *Margins of Philosophy*, translated by Alan Bass. Chicago: University of Chicago Press, 1982, 1–27.

Eagleton, Terry. *Literary Theory: An Introduction.* Minneapolis: University of Minnesota Press, 1983.

———. *Ideology: An Introduction.* London: Verso, 1991.

"Editorial Statement." *Cultural Studies* 10 (1996).

Ellis, John. *The Theory of Literary Criticism: A Logical Analysis.* Berkeley: University of California Press, 1974.

Elmer, Jonathan, and Cary Wolfe. "Subject or Sacrifice: Ideology, Psychoanalysis, and the Discourse of Species in Jonathan Demme's *Silence of the Lambs.*" *boundary 2* 22 (1995), 141–70.

Erkkila, Betsy. "Whitman and American Empire." In *Walt Whitman of Mickle Street: A Centennial Collection*, edited by Geoffrey M. Sill. Knoxville: University of Tennessee Press, 1994, 54–69.

Ernest, John. "Economies of Identity: Harriet E. Wilson's *Our Nig.*" *PMLA* 109 (1994), 424–38.

Felski, Rita. *The Gender of Modernity.* Cambridge, MA: Harvard University Press, 1995.

Ferguson, Priscilla Parkhurst, Philippe Desan, and Wendy Griswold. "Introduction." "The Sociology of Literature," special issue of *Critical Inquiry* 14 (1988), 421–30.

Fish, Stanley. *Professional Correctness: Literary Studies and Political Change.* Oxford: Clarendon Press, 1995.

"Forum on Interdisciplinarity." *PMLA* 111 (1996), 271–311.

Foucault, Michel. *The Archaeology of Knowledge and The Discourse on Language*, translated by A. M. Sheridan Smith. New York: Pantheon Books, 1972.

———. *Language, Counter-Memory, Practice*, translated by Donald F. Bouchard and Sherry Simon, edited by Donald F. Bouchard. Ithaca, NY: Cornell University Press, 1977.

Fuss, Diana. *Essentially Speaking: Feminism, Nature, and Difference.* New York and London: Routledge, 1989.

Garber, Marjorie. "The Logic of the Transvestite: *The Roaring Girl* (1608)." In *Staging the Renaissance: Reinterpretations of Elizabethan and Jacobean Drama*, edited by David Scott Kastan and Peter Stallybrass. New York: Routledge, 1991, 221–34.

Geertz, Clifford. *The Interpretation of Cultures*. New York: Basic Books, 1973.
———. "Blurred Genres: The Refiguration of Social Thought." *American Scholar* 49 (1980), 165–79.
———. *Local Knowledge: Further Essays in Interpretive Anthropology*. New York: Basic Books, 1983.
Giroux, Henry A. "Consuming Social Change: The 'United Colors of Benetton.'" *Cultural Critique* 23 (1993–94), 5–32.
Graff, Gerald. "Determinacy/Indeterminacy." In *Critical Terms for Literary Study*, edited by Frank Lentricchia and Thomas McLaughlin. Chicago: University of Chicago Press, 1990, 163–76.
Greenblatt, Stephen J. *Learning to Curse: Essays in Early Modern Culture*. New York: Routledge, 1990.
———. "The Eating of the Soul." *Representations* 48 (1994), 97–116.
Groden, Michael, and Martin Kreiswirth, editors. *The Johns Hopkins Guide to Literary Theory and Criticism*. Foreword by Richard Macksey. Baltimore: Johns Hopkins University Press, 1994.
Grossberg, Lawrence, Cary Nelson, and Paula Treichler, editors. *Cultural Studies*. London and New York: Routledge, 1992.
Guillory, John. "Canon." In *Critical Terms for Literary Study*, edited by Frank Lentricchia and Thomas McLaughlin. Chicago: University of Chicago Press, 1990, 233–249.
———. *Cultural Capital: The Problem of Literary Canon Formation*. Chicago: University of Chicago Press, 1993.
Haraway, Donna. "The Biopolitics of Postmodern Bodies: Determinations of Self in Immune System Discourse." *Differences* 1 (1989), 3–43.
Heidegger, Martin. *Being and Time*, translated by John Macquarrie and Edward Robinson. New York: Harper and Row, 1962.
Hutcheon, Linda. "The Postmodern Problematizing of History." *Review of English Studies in Canada* 14 (1988), 364–82.
Interdisciplinarity: Problems of Teaching and Research in Universities. Paris: Organization for Economic Co-operation and Development, 1972.
Kallberg, Jeffrey. "The Harmony of the Tea Table: Gender and Ideology in the Piano Nocturne." *Representations* 39 (1992), 102–33.
Klein, Julie Thompson. *Interdisciplinarity: History, Theory, Practice*. Detroit: Wayne State University Press, 1990.
Kockelmans, Joseph J. "Science and Discipline: Some Historical and Critical Reflections." In *Interdisciplinarity and Higher Education*, edited by Joseph J. Kockelmans. University Park: Pennsylvania State University Press, 1979, 11–48.
Kolodny, Annette. "Inventing a Feminist Discourse: Rhetoric and Resistance in Margaret Fuller's *Woman in the Nineteenth Century*." *New Literary History* 25 (1994), 355–82.
Lentricchia, Frank. *Criticism and Social Change*. Chicago: University of Chicago Press, 1983.
Loesberg, Jonathan. "The Ideology of Narrative Form in Sensation Fiction." *Representations* 13 (1986), 115–38.
Marx, Karl, and Friedrich Engels. *The Marx-Engels Reader*, edited by Robert C. Tucker. New York: W. W. Norton, 1972.

McGann, Jerome J. *The Romantic Ideology: A Critical Investigation.* Chicago and London: University of Chicago Press, 1983.

Merod, Jim. *The Political Responsibility of the Critic.* Ithaca, NY and London: Cornell University Press, 1987.

Miller, D. A. "*Cages aux Folles*: Sensation and Gender in Wilkie Collins's *The Woman in White.*" In *Speaking of Gender*, edited by Elaine Showalter. New York: Routledge, 1989, 187–215.

Mohanty, Satya P. "Colonial Legacies, Multicultural Futures: Relativism, Objectivity, and the Challenge of Otherness." *PMLA* 110 (1995), 108–18.

Moi, Toril. "Ambiguity and Alienation in *The Second Sex.*" *boundary 2* 19 (1992), 96–112.

Montrose, Louis. "The Work of Gender and the Discourse of Discovery." *Representations* 33 (1991), 1–41.

Norris, Christopher. *The Contest of Faculties: Philosophy and Theory After Deconstruction.* London and New York: Methuen, 1985.

Parsons, Talcott. "Theory in the Humanities and Sociology." *Daedalus* 99 (1970), 495–523.

Plotnisky, Arkady. "The Medusa's Ears: The Question of Nietzsche, the Question of Gender, and Transformations of Theory." In *Nietzsche and the Feminine*, edited by Peter J. Burgard. Charlottesville: University Press of Virginia, 1994, 230–53.

Poster, Mark. "The Question of Agency: Michel de Certeau and the History of Consumerism." *Diacritics* 22 (1992), 4–107.

Potkay, Adam. "Virtue and Manners in Macpherson's *Poems of Ossian.*" *PMLA* 107 (1992), 120–130.

Preminger, Alex, T. V. F. Brogan, et al., editors. *The New Princeton Encyclopedia of Poetry and Poetics.* Princeton, NJ: Princeton University Press, 1993.

Preziosi, Donald. *Rethinking Art History: Meditations on a Coy Science.* New Haven, CT and London: Yale University Press, 1989.

Prince, Gerald. *A Dictionary of Narratology.* Lincoln and London: University of Nebraska Press, 1987.

Przybylowicz, Donna, Nancy Hartsock, and Pamela McCallum, editors. "The Construction of Gender and Modes of Social Division." Special issues of *Cultural Critique* 13 and 14 (1989–90).

Rawson, Claude. "'Indians' and Irish: Montaigne, Swift, and the Cannibal Question." *MLQ* 53 (1992), 299–363.

Reising, Russell. "Lionel Trilling, *The Liberal Imagination*, and the Emergence of the Cultural Discourse of Anti-Stalinism." *boundary 2* 20 (1993), 94–124.

Richards, I. A. *Practical Criticism: A Study of Literary Judgment.* New York: Routledge, 1964.

Robbins, Bruce. "Death and Vocation: Narrativizing Narrative Theory." *PMLA* 107 (1992), 38–50.

Ryan, Judith. "More Seductive than Phryne: Baudelaire, Gerome, Rilke, and the Problem of Autonomous Art." *PMLA* 108 (1993), 1128–41.

Said, Edward W. *The World, the Text, the Critic.* Cambridge, MA: Harvard University Press, 1983.

Scholes, Robert. *Textual Power: Literary Theory and the Teaching of English.* New Haven, CT: Yale University Press, 1985.

Scott, Joan Wallach. *Gender and the Politics of History.* New York: Columbia University Press, 1988.

Sedgwick, Eve Kosofsky. "Across Gender, Across Sexuality: Willa Cather and Others." *South Atlantic Quarterly* 88 (1989), 53–72.

———. *Epistemology of the Closet.* Berkeley: University of California Press, 1990.

Silverman, Kaja. *Male Subjectivity at the Margins.* New York: Routledge, 1992.

Spillers, Hortense. "Mama's Baby, Papa's Maybe: An American Grammar Book." *Diacritics* 19 (1987), 65–81.

Spivak, Gayatri Chakravorty. *The Post-Colonial Critic: Interviews, Strategies, Dialogues,* edited by Sarah Harasym. New York and London: Routledge, 1990.

Stimpson, Catherine R. "The Somagrams of Gertrude Stein." In *The Female Body in Western Culture: Contemporary Perspectives,* edited by Susan Rubin Suleiman. Cambridge, MA: Harvard University Press, 1986, 30–43.

Weber, Samuel. *Institution and Interpretation.* Minneapolis: University of Minnesota Press, 1987.

Williams, Raymond. *The Country and the City.* New York: Oxford University Press, 1973.

———. *Keywords: A Vocabulary of Culture and Society.* New York: Oxford University Press, 1985.

Wolfson, Susan. "*Lyrical Ballads* and the Language of (Men) Feeling: Writing Women's Voices." In *Men Writing the Feminine: Literature, Theory, and the Question of Genders,* edited by Thais E. Morgan. Albany: State University of New York Press, 1994, 29–57.

Index